"Pink Elephant In The Middle of the Getto"

My Journey Through Childhood Molestation, Mental Illness, Addiction and Healing

By: TiTi Ladette

This is a work of non-fiction. Although the names of
characters, and some of the circumstances have ben
changed, the book is based on the real life of TiTi Ladette.

Edited By: Rose Smith

This book is dedicated to the three most influential men in my life: My grandfather, J.D. Cleveland, my father W.J. Cleveland, and my brother, D.R. Cleveland.

It is a special tribute to my children; whom I love with everything inside me.

Also for my best friend, Twayler, the man of my dreams, Vincent,
and for Jamie Shaw, the man who told me in spite of my past, I can do whatever I set my mind to.

A Note to My Family

When I was a child, I talked like a child; I thought like a child, I reasoned like a child. When I grew up, I put away childish things.

1ˢᵗ Corinthians 13:11
New Living Translation

To My Loving Family,

I guess I want you all to know that this book is not some "tell–all" in which I wish to air our dirty laundry publically. It is the story of my life in which I must tell to find inner peace. Although the names and some details have been changed to protect members of our family; it is the truth as I know it.

For many years, I viewed the incidents in this book in a child-like manner, with a child-like mind. But, as an adult, I understand that people have done the best they could with what they had. I also know today that no one meant to damage me, and had no idea that some of the words that were said to me would scar me for life.

I know today that you truly love me. You have proved it by taking in my children when I couldn't take care of them, by being there for me financially when times were rough, but mostly by supporting my dreams today.

I have always loved my family, and it is only today that I realize that you all love me just as much.

Thanks for not giving up on me, even when I gave up on myself. Thanks for loving me, even when I wasn't lovable. But most importantly, thank you all for continuing to keep me in your prayers.

With Love,

TiTi

Foreword

How gratifying and refreshing it is to witness a portrait of stability, struggle and grace. We are given the opportunity to view the making of a masterpiece in the writing of this epic autobiography of TiTi Ladette. Windows are strategically designed by the architect for the purpose of displaying a "would be" hidden feature of a structure. We are able to look into the window of the various challenges and hardships of this great author. She exposes her pain to the world and without shame, shares the heartbreak and tribulations of her journey in hopes that it may strengthen those who are yet seeking guidance and understanding.

Not only will this book give direction but it will also outline resources that will empower parents, children, educators with not only the ability to identify those who are in desperate need for help, but also those who seek to rise above this obstruction of liberty. The overall purpose of this book is to provide assistance for those who have been unnecessarily scarred without cause and have learned to exchange their garments of shame into garments of praise.

Every "getto" has a pink elephant, but not many live to tell their story. Embrace the heart of this author and emancipate yourself from the jungle of your past. It gives me great honor to present this fine piece of literature from one who has conquered the assailants of yesterday. Be enriched, encouraged and engaged.

Edward M. Fleming , Sr.

There's a pink elephant in the middle of the ghetto

It has many names and faces

Names like molestation, addiction, and mental illness

Found in the ghetto of all places

Does anyone see this pink elephant?

Do they even know it's there?

Are they too consumed with image that no one seems to care?

It's time to do something about the elephant

If we don't it's sure to kill

For those of us who've been hurt but aren't dead

It's definitely time to heal.

-TiTi Ladette

PROLOGUE

I don't know exactly what woke me. I blinked several times in an attempt to adjust my eyes to the darkness. The only light was the glow of a street lamp through the bedroom window. Slowly my eyes adjusted to my familiar surroundings; the mix matched worn furniture in the bedroom I shared with my sisters and two aunts. My two sisters and I shared a twin bed, and so did my aunts. My sister Yvette and I slept towards the head of the bed, my sister Amber towards the foot. My two aunts, Yolanda and Denice, also slept in a similar fashion on the other side of the room.

My eyes seemed to focus on a strange sight. The glow from the outside street lamp illuminated what appeared to be a white tee shirt hovering over the end of the bed where my sister slept. Knowing that made no sense, I focused even harder until the vision became clear. As far as I could tell, there was someone bent over my sister kissing her deeply in her mouth and the cover was moving up and down....down there between her legs. It took several moments for my 5 year old brain to compute and decipher what it was I was actually seeing. When it dawned on me that I was actually seeing someone bent over my sister kissing her and touching her between her legs, I became very frightened and began to call for my Grandmother whom I called "Mamma."

I must have whispered it or said it really low the first couple of times, because whomever was bent over my sister didn't budge, nor were they fazed by me calling for my

Grandmother. I remember calling my Grandmother louder and louder, "Mamma, Mamma, Mamma" Suddenly, they heard me and bolted out of our room to the back of the house. There were only two other rooms in the back of our house which were my Uncle Haywood's room and the bathroom. I knew the indistinguishable person had to be my Uncle Haywood because I stayed up all night after the incident, and no one ever came from the back of the house.

The next morning, the first chance I got, I cornered my grandmother and told her in no uncertain terms that Uncle Haywood had done some nasty, bad things to my sister the night before. I explicitly shared with my grandmother how he kissed her in the mouth and touched her "down there." Although I was five years old, my grandmother knew exactly what I was telling her. She nodded her head knowingly and told me not to worry and she said that she would take care of it.

I was happy that day. I knew my grandmother would probably put my uncle out of the house and my sisters and I could go back to feeling secure and protected and being happy- go- lucky kids. However, that evening, all I heard was my grandmother fussing at my uncle, telling him that he knew better than to be "messing with his niece". There was no major quarreling, no emptying of closets or drawers, simply a "you know better than that" or two, and that was it.

From that day on and for the next five years, my uncle never came into our room again. Instead….he took my sister, Amber, in the bathroom every night.

Chapter 1

THE BEGINNING

"The beginning cannot be changed because it is the past, but you can always rewrite the ending."

-TiTi Ladette

I was raised by my paternal grandparents in a small, Black community called St. John's. In our community, the inhabitants practically lived by the motto "It takes a village to raise a child." Everyone knew each other by name. If you passed by Miss So-n-So's house and didn't respectfully speak, it was known by your parents by the time you made it home. Of course, this was a serious infraction, and was often punishable by a whooping. It was also known by Miss So-n-So when this had been addressed, because the next time you passed by her house, she was greeted loudly and intentionally.

My grandparents raised my brother Ernest and two sisters, Yvette, Amber and myself, along with their own ten children; most of whom were already grown and living with their spouses. I was seven months old when I came to live with my grandparents. Ernest and Yvette, who are twins, were two years old and Amber was 3 years old. Needless to say, I was the baby and boy was I spoiled. I slept in the bed with my grandparents until I was four years old, and would often cry in the middle of the night for a glass of milk. I was overweight, and the doctor put me on a "no milk" diet. But, my grandmother, not wanting to hear my crying, would often quietly consent and give me milk. Nevertheless, I felt safe and secure during my beginning years.

I was very intelligent as a child. Ernest would come home from school and teach me everything he learned throughout his kindergarten, first and second grade years. As a result, by the time I made it to kindergarten, I already knew how to read. I thrived in school, exuberant in my new learning environment. I made really good grades, and always participated in class. Up until the age of five, I was happy and fun loving, without a care in the world. Those first five years would be the last carefree years I would know.

Shortly after my uncle Haywood began taking my sister, Amber, in the bathroom at night, she'd get into our small bed and cuddle up to me. This would eventually turn into her hunching and feeling on me, and wanting to kiss and embrace me for long periods of time. Although I was only five at the time, I knew in my young mind that she was only doing to me what was being done to her. I could remember feeling sorry for my sister. So sorry, in fact, that I would allow her to hump, kiss, and rub on me although I knew it was wrong. This would be my first experience with feeling sorry for someone else at my own expense. Coincidentally, this is where I developed my first concept of love. I thought love meant that I was supposed to let others do what they wanted to do to me while I suffered silently.

Religion and church were a top priority in our house. My grandfather was the epitome of the southern Black preacher. He pastored not one, but two churches that alternated services every other Sunday. My grandfather was definitely the "fire and brimstone" type of preacher that took the Bible at its most literal meaning. Especially the verse about "Spare the rod, spoil the child." We were abused by today's standards, but back then it was considered a "whooping" and there was no recourse. No social worker, no friendly police officer...just the "whooping."

Whoopings in the Black community were usually meted with an object. A belt, an extension cord, or a piece of toy race track, but in our case, we were whooped with a razor strap. These are the thick pieces of metal enlaced leather straps that barbers sharpen their razors on.

My grandfather wasn't a huge man, but he had broad shoulders and he was as strong as an ox. He would often beat us until he got tired. He didn't curse, but he had a way of talking to you that would make you shrink. I used to think he was the meanest man in the world, and I would pee my pants every time I got a whooping. For that matter, I would pee in my pants every time he called my name. And, because I would wet myself, I would often get back to back whoopings.

For the life of me, I couldn't figure out why this God that my grandfather preached about would let me get beat this way. I was taught that God loves us, but would send you to hell if you were bad. So early on I thought that I was bad because I was constantly being beaten and those beatings hurt. But, where was God when my uncle was being bad towards my sister? Where was God when my grandfather was beating us? Wasn't it bad to hurt people? I waited every day for God to send us all to hell.

Around this time, I found out that my grandparents were not my birth parents. My two younger aunts were resentful when my brother, sister, and I came to live with them and they were the ones who told me that my grandparents were not really my parents. They were often mean to us and would tease us and taunt us. They would say things like

"This isn't really your food," or "You guys are really orphans," or even worse, "Your daddy is sorry."

This bothered and affected me deeply. I begin to resent them. And, I made a vow that I would never put myself in the position to have to ask anybody for anything, especially food. I began asking my grandmother questions about my mother and father. My grandmother would always give these spiritual answers. When I would ask about my mother, my grandmother would say "She died of a heart attack, let her rest in peace." When I would ask why my father couldn't take care of us, she would say, "He's getting himself together."

The fact that God took my mother away confirmed the fact that I was bad. In my mind, I thought I didn't deserve to have a mother like everyone else.

Fantasy became my best friend. I would sit and fantasize for hours and hours about my real parents, and why we were left with my grandparents. The best fantasy I came up with was that my father was involved in the mafia and wanted to get out. So, they killed my mother, and were actually looking for us (my brother, sisters, and I) so my father hid us in a different city with his elderly parents.

Because I fantasized and talked about my fantasies so much, I was quickly labeled as a "story teller" by my family members. We weren't allowed to say "liar." In my fantasy world, I was always the heroine. I would save everyone from sudden death or become rich and famous and give everyone money. I was always loved and wanted in my fantasies. It certainly didn't feel that I was loved and wanted in real life.

Around the age of six, I began to develop my sense of self-esteem. I began to notice differences between myself and others. One of the most esteem defining moments of my life was when my aunt Dorothy, whom I thought was the most beautiful member of my family, announced that she was getting married. This aunt was light-skinned. And, she wore her make up perfectly and always dressed nice. She was the pianist at our church, and she became engaged to a light- skinned, handsome singer in the choir. Skin color was epic to me because I was dark-skinned with short, nappy hair. Although I wasn't the only dark-skinned person in the family, everyone else had long, pretty hair, even the boys. I wore short afro puffs.

I clearly remember when my aunt Dorothy announced her engagement at choir rehearsal. My two cousins, Paulette and Lisa were around the same age as I. Paulette was a couple of years younger than Lisa and I, but we often played together. When my aunt announced her engagement, Lisa and I began running around the church chanting, "We're going to be flower girls! We're going to be flower girls…"

Everyone was so excited, especially me. I couldn't wait to put on a frilly dress and sprinkle flower petals down the aisle as I'd seen flower girls at other weddings do. I would for the next few months, practice throwing flowers and smiling at wedding guests.

I remember the day I found out that I would not be a flower girl. Instead, Paulette and Lisa had been chosen to be the flower girls. I knew immediately it was because they were light-skinned with long hair, and that they could wear the decorations in their hair. I felt ugly and awkward. But, more than anything, I was ashamed and embarrassed because I had run through the church singing to everyone that I was going to be a flower girl.

My grandmother tried to appease me by buying me a new dress for the wedding. My aunt tried to appease me by making me a junior usher in her wedding, but nothing worked. In fact, I got a whooping the day of the wedding for "showing out." Truth was, I didn't want to go to the wedding at all. My tape was created that day....the tape that would play in my head for the next thirty five years. "I'm not good enough, and everybody knows it."

Being raised in the home of a preacher had its drawbacks. We couldn't go to parties, sleepovers, or have friends sleep over. At bed time, our grandfather would hit the main power breaker and all the power in our house would go out. Everything would be black and silent, and if you weren't already in bed you'd have to grope around in the dark until you found your way to your bed. On the upswing, we got to have the latest fashions and were always dressed better than our classmates and adolescent church members because as my grandmother would huff, "Ain't nobody gon' be talking about us!"

Church attendance was non-negotiable. We had to attend church whether we were sick, tired, or otherwise. I remember one Sunday my sister Yvette pretended to have lost her church shoes; trying to get out of going to church. After much fussing by my grandfather, he decided to get a cardboard and some string. He traced her feet on the cardboard, cut around them, and poked holes for the string that would be laced up her legs. My sister quickly found her shoes.

We didn't receive a lot of affection growing up. The only way you knew you were loved is because you were fed, clothed, and had a roof over your head. There were no hugs and kisses, no "I love you" or terms of endearment. This also created an issue with me because I would watch TV shows like "Goodtimes" or "What's Happening," and the mother always said "I love you" at some point in the show. They also always talked at the dinner table. This just didn't happen in our home. I always felt that if I had my real, young parents instead of my elderly grandparents, my life would resemble the lives of the characters on the TV shows.

We did hear from our dad occasionally, mostly Christmas or a birthday. We saw him every few years or so. One year he called for my birthday asking me what I wanted. I was so excited. I knew exactly what I wanted. I asked him for a Barbie Doll Dream House. When the doll house arrived through the mail; I was very disappointed. I barely wanted to talk to him on the phone or thank him for sending it.

He asked me what was wrong and I had to be honest and tell him the dollhouse he sent was not a Barbie doll dream house. In fact, it was so tiny that my Barbie dolls couldn't even fit in it. I felt bad for him because I knew he felt bad, but I couldn't hide my disappointment. A few months later he called and asked what I wanted for Christmas. Not wanting to set myself up again, I mentioned that whatever he bought me would be fine.

Lo and behold, on Christmas morning, I un-wrapped the three-sectional, elevator-to-the-top, Barbie Doll Dream House! That was my favorite Christmas as a child, and one I will always remember. It was the first time I'd gotten exactly what I wanted. The gift tag read "To: Baby Girl From: Daddy and Karen." Of course, we all wanted to know who Karen was. Judging by the gifts that were sent that year, whoever she was, she was needed!

When I was nine years old I met Karen for the first time. My uncle and aunt drove us to Houston, Texas to see our father and meet Karen. She was very nice to us. She had five kids of her own. But, she treated us like we were her kids, and that she had known us all of our lives. This would prove to be monumental in my life because it fulfilled my fantasy, to have a mother. Karen obviously received the stamp of approval from my uncle and aunt, because we were allowed to spend the summer of my eleventh birthday in Houston with Karen and our father. It was the best summer of my life. My sisters and I were allowed to go to work with Karen, who managed a dry cleaners, while my brother would go to work with our father who did carpentry/handyman work. Karen taught us to pull tickets, cashier, and greet customers. We had a tip jar and always got lots of tips from the customers. Best of all, when the regular customers would ask Karen who we were, she always introduced us as her daughters. In the evening, my sisters and I would argue with my brother about who worked the hardest, and we'd all share stories about our work day. We got along great with Karen's five sons. We always considered ourselves to be brothers and sisters. Karen also had a daughter that died a couple of months before we arrived that summer while giving birth to a baby girl. Before we left Houston for the summer, Karen and our dad piled all us kids in the car and took us for a ride. They told us they had a surprise for us. We'd spent the entire summer in Houston, and it was the longest time we'd ever spent with our father. We couldn't think of a better surprise than that.

They drove us a few blocks and pulled in front of a two story house. They told us they hoped we all liked the house because when school starts we would be coming back to Houston, and this is where we were all going to live. Plus, they were getting married. We were all hugging, screaming and cheering and were so excited. I went back to Austin feeling better than I ever had about my circumstances.

I had a connection with my father that was unbelievable. Everyone in my family is musically inclined, especially my father. He could play any instrument he picked up. His favorite was lead guitar. He often played his guitar for us late in the evening and we would listen as if at a concert. Once I got on his piano and picked out a song. My father was so excited. He told me I had the Cleveland gift. We actually wrote a short song together. I will never forget sitting at the piano with my father. Since I was his youngest, I knew I was his pick and he spoiled me and made me feel special. He would look at me like I was the most important thing in his world. For the first time ever, I felt loved and wanted.

When we got back to our grandparent's home, we were excited about going back to Houston. But our grandparents were struggling with the decision of letting us move with our father. We were not only raised by our grandparents, they legally adopted us and became our guardians. And, they took their legal obligation seriously.

School had begun and we were sad. We were hoping to start the school year in Houston with our father and Karen. One evening, we got a call from our father. He said he and Karen were still working on getting us down there but in the meantime he had something he wanted to discuss with the four of us. During his conversation with me, I thought it was strange because he wasn't talking to me like he would see me soon. He was talking like he wouldn't see me again. He told me to do really good in school and to always obey my grandparents. He told my brother to watch out for me and my sisters. I hung up with him feeling depressed, dejected and not sure of anything.

We went about our school week as usual. And, the next Sunday, one of my aunts went into labor so the adults left church, to go to the hospital. They left all the kids at my grandparent's house with my two older aunts. We were all running around playing hide and seek when the phone rang. The main aunt who loved to tell us how sorry our daddy was took the phone call. She started screaming, crying, and pulling at her hair. No one could make sense of what she was saying. For some reason, I knew it had something to do with my father.

When my grandparents drove up to tell us our aunt delivered a baby boy, my aunt ran to the car screaming, "William's dead! William's dead!"

At first, I was too stunned to cry. I remember feeling very numb, and in my heart I knew it happened because I was bad and this was God's way of punishing me. For days I walked around not really knowing how to feel. I would cry a little, but I remember that I would not eat. I was emotionally in turmoil. On one hand, I really didn't know my father, but on the other hand I felt a strong connection with him. How could he enter my life only to leave it? I became angry with God.

The next few days were a blur. I was bought a new dress to wear to my father's funeral, and I remembered thinking that even at a time like this, my grandparents wanted us to look our best. I learned in that moment to dress up the outside even when the inside is a mess.

After the funeral, things began to change with me. I had never really been a child who acted out, but I began to talk back to my grandparents and misbehave at school. This led to more beatings with the razor strap, but I didn't care. I became immune to the beatings.

One thing I knew without a shadow of a doubt was that I was bad and not good enough. That's why God took away my parents. That's why I got horrible beatings. That's why my hair was short and nappy. But, mainly, that's why no one loved me or wanted me. I was bad. So, I might as well act like it.

Chapter 2

Molestation

"Who knows what evil lurks in the heart of men? The shadow knows..."

- Dark Shadow

After the death of my father, I went buck wild. I began to notice my body and how it was developing. I had small, perky breasts, a thin waist, and thick, muscular legs. What I was really waiting on was the thing I thought would make me a real woman…..my period. We learned about it in health class, and most of my friends already had theirs. I felt left out and different, and did not like the feeling. My sister had long since started her period, so I used to sneak her pads, and go in the bathroom to put them on. They were pretty uncomfortable and I didn't see the big deal about wearing them, but none the less, I was very ready to start.

Once, my grandmother caught me wearing a pad. She was so "old school," that she never sat us down and talked to us about the changes our bodies would go through. She never talked about our periods or sex. When she caught me wearing the pad, she just asked if I needed some of those. I was embarrassed, so I lied and said yes.

As I said, lying and fantasy was my friend. In reality, there was a lot of speculation about my father's death. Although I was a child, I would over hear my aunts talking to Karen about what happened. The story has it that my father was working in a woman's attic, when his sweaty neck touched a live wire and he was accidentally electrocuted. In my fantasy, the mafia finally found my father and killed him. I began believing my own lies. I began telling this story to all my classmates and people who asked about my parents. No adults ever believed me, but they never called me on it.

Shortly after my father's death, I began to venture away from home, and I would sneak and smoke my grandfather's cigarettes. I would walk a couple of blocks to a street where no one who knew me could call my grandparents. And, I would smoke. One day a lady, named Regina saw me smoking and told me to come here. I just knew I was in trouble. I was relieved when she asked if I wouldn't mind watching her small kids for a moment while she ran to the store. She told me she would leave me three cigarettes so I said okay. I felt like an adult. She even let me smoke the cigarettes in her house. She came back an hour later, gave me two more cigarettes and two dollars. This became a daily ritual.

I don't know why, but no one questioned my whereabouts during this time. As long as I was home before the street lights came on, I was allowed to "go play" in the neighborhood after homework and chores were done.

One evening I was babysitting Regina's children, I noticed it was getting later and later and she still had not returned home, so I started getting worried. I didn't want to leave her kids alone, but I knew I had to get home before it got dark. Finally, she came in. She gave me two dollars, two cigarettes and went straight into the bathroom as she usually did. She called my name and told me to come into the bathroom just as I was about to walk out the door. I became apprehensive because she'd never done that. Every time she came in from "the store" she'd come in, pay me, go to the bathroom, and then yell bye from there. When I opened the bathroom door, she was sitting in the bathtub with the water running. The bathtub was halfway filled with water. Apparently, she shaved her vagina, as there was pubic hair floating in the water, and all I could think of was "how disgusting!"

She called me over to the bathroom, and although I was hesitant, I went anyway. After all, she was an adult and I was taught to obey and respect all adults. So, when she asked for my arm, I obediently stuck it out. She quickly injected a needle filled with cocaine in my arm. It happened so quickly I didn't have a chance to object or voice my fear of needles.

As soon as the drug entered my blood stream, a feeling of blissful euphoria washed over me and the whole world seemed brighter and more beautiful. Even the hair floating in the bathtub was beautiful.

Seeing my reaction to the drug, Regina stood up in the bathtub and guided my hand between her legs. I felt as if I were in a dream. She asked me if I knew what the little man in the boat was. I told her I didn't. She explained to me that it was my clitoris, and she skinned her labia back to show me hers. She told me that if I wanted to make her happy, I should lick and suck on it. So I did. Again, I thought this was the most beautiful thing in the world. Her body was severely scarred and marred with needle marks and wounds, but because of the effects of the drug it was beautiful to me also.

When I finally made it home, nobody asked where I'd been or if I was ok, or if anything had happened to me. My grandfather just pulled me in the house by my head and whooped me until I peed my pants for coming in after the street lights came on.

At this time, I am thirteen years old and in junior high school. I felt so different from my peers. I had a cigarette habit, I'd had sex with a woman and never with a boy, and I still hadn't had my period. I felt old beyond my years. I felt that the rest of my classmates were babies and didn't know half of what I knew.

Around this time I met two girls in school named Monica and Michelle. They were very cool because they also smoked cigarettes. Monica was skinny as a rail and quite possibly the skinniest person I'd ever met. Michelle was the total opposite. She was HUGE. I was somewhere in between. They introduced me to marijuana and acid. Every time I smoked a joint, it brought up the euphoric feelings of "beauty" and "escape." I always wanted to feel that way. When I was high, I forgot I was dark with nappy hair. I felt beautiful and sexy. I would forget the pain and misery I felt from not having parents, and living in a place where I felt I was eating someone else's food that was being bought by someone else's parents. I loved the feeling of being high. Soon I began skipping school and hanging out with older people at a place called "Martin's Drive Inn." It was located on the East Side of Austin.

It was a dark, dank hole-in-the-wall where pimps, prostitutes and con artists hung out. I remember the prostitutes smelling like musk and sex, wearing wigs and a bunch of make up and wearing skimpy clothes. Because of the drugs in my system, this would all seem glamorous to me and all I could think of was wanting to do what they were doing. I wanted lots of men to tell me how beautiful I was. The prostitutes always had lots of money and drugs and I thought that was the life.

Pretty soon, I quit hanging with Monica and Michelle altogether. All of a sudden, they didn't seem as old as I was. Both of them were actually older than me. But, I was hanging with a much older crowd and I couldn't be seen hanging with babies. Going to Martin's Drive Inn, getting loaded, and watching the prostitutes and pimps was my daily ritual.

One day I met a guy they called Pretty Tony. He was probably twenty-two or twenty-three years old. At the time I was fourteen. He was my first real sexual experience with a man. The year before my brother gave a condom to his best friend to have sex with me after school one day, but he was inexperienced and I don't think he even penetrated me. Pretty Tony was different. He broke my cherry. We did it in the back seat of his car and after he finished he asked me if I liked it. I lied and said yes. In truth, I just liked the idea of him making all the noises and telling me how good I was. He told me that the next time I wanted him to do that to me I would have to pay for it. Like a fool, I asked him how much it cost. Little did I know he was a pimp about to turn me out.

During this time, I was caught in a vicious cycle. I would skip school, smoke weed all day and have sex with random men for money. Then I would go home, do my chores and be a kid. Once a month, I would get the stuffing beat out of me because the school would notify my grandparents about my absences. But, I was smart, and I would always manage to catch up on the school work or ace the tests in order to pass to the next grade.

My last year in junior high school, while we were out of school for winter break, my brother, sister, and I went to stay with my maternal aunt. We often visited my aunt on my mother's side of the family, but I always felt funny around her. She had married into money and always considered herself to be above everyone else. Her daughter and I were the same age and got along really well as kids, but she was a tattle tale. My mother's side of the family seemed to think they were classier than my father's side of the family so I always felt I had to put on airs around them.

One day during our break, my cousin and I went for a walk in their neighborhood. There were some guys standing outside a duplex hanging out. They were way older, so my cousin wanted to keep walking. I, of course, wanted to stop and talk to them. She won. But, when we got back to my aunt's house, I took off on a bicycle and went back around the corner where the guys were.

They were outside smoking cigarettes, so I rolled up and asked for one. I impressed them all by actually inhaling the smoke like a professional. One of the guys introduced his self and we instantly hit it off. He told me he was twenty years old and asked me if I believed in love at first sight. His name was Vandeline, but everyone called him Van. I was in love for the first time in my life. We exchanged phone numbers, and I started going over to his house when I skipped school instead of going to Martin's Drive Inn to whore. Coincidentally, during this time, I'd finally gotten my period. I was hoping to get pregnant by him so that I could be with him and not have to sneak. I told Van I was seventeen. He had no idea I was only fourteen.

One day my cousin asked where I went when I skipped school. I told her I would go to Van's house. The next time I skipped school, my aunt drove right up to Van's house. Van had a room at his brother's place and this particular day we had just got out of the bed and got dressed when my aunt knocked at the door.

She and my uncle were livid. They explained to Van and his brother that I was fourteen years old and if she caught us together again, she would file statutory rape on him. As we drove away she asked me several questions. Every answer I would give her, she would slap me in my mouth and tell me to stop lying. She explained to me what statutory rape was and told me Van could go to jail for a long time for it. I couldn't imagine not seeing him again.

I waited for a week, and then skipped school again. I went to Van's brother's house and knocked on the door. His brother answered the door and told me that Van had gotten a job and was at work. I turned and walked away, but I knew in my heart that Van was in the house. I walked down the street with nowhere to go feeling once again unloved and unwanted. I knew that Van loved me for who I was and not because of my body.

As I neared the next block, a chunky Mexican guy in a van pulled over and offered me a ride. I got in and he took me to his house where we had sex and he fed me lunch. Later that afternoon, he took me to meet the school bus. I had just got out of the van, and was walking toward the bus stop when my aunt pulls up. She had received a call from the school that I had skipped and boy was she mad! She accused me of being somewhere with Van (she'd obviously been by his house first) but couldn't prove it. I finally convinced her that I wasn't with Van. She told me she didn't care who I'd been with, we were going to the police department.

When we got there my aunt spoke to a detective and explained to him that I'd been skipping school having sex with older guys. The detective wanted names and specific sexual information. I knew that I couldn't let them arrest Van, so I told the detective I was having sex with Pretty Tony and that he was my pimp. Pretty Tony was a well-known pimp, and they had his mug shot from a prior conviction. I picked him out of a photo lineup and made a statement. Since they kept using the terms "rape," "incident," and "suspect," I ran with it. I became really dramatic and came up with this elaborate story that Pretty Tony physically raped me and made me whore for him. I said he forced me to get in the car with him, and he held me down and let other men sleep with me for money. I also told the detective that he threatened to kill me and my family members if I ever told anyone. Of course, most of this was untrue. I rationalized sending him to jail because although this was a made up story, he really was having sex with me and pimping me.

After this, I became really depressed. Van stopped taking my phone calls, and the next time I went by his brother's place, the house was empty. They had moved.

I came in, went into my grandparent's medicine cabinet and took a bottle full of pills in an attempt to kill myself. I was rushed to the hospital where they pumped my stomach, and made me drink gallons of black tar. The doctors recommended I be admitted to the State hospital. My grandparents were at an absolute loss as what to do with me and my out of control behavior. So, they had me committed. This would be my introduction to institutionalized living.

When I first arrived in the state hospital, they placed me in the Psychiatric Intensive Care Unit (PICU), which is where all the newly admitted patients go. I was very upset. This is where the "real crazy" people are housed and although I was a lot of things, I wasn't crazy. I soon found out that I would only have to be in PICU for a couple of days for observation and then would be classified to a regular unit.

After a few days I was sent to a regular unit. There were other teenagers there who had problems similar to mine. There were runaways, cutters, addicts, and the like. I was the only Black girl there at the time, so I learned to like rock music, speak proper, and basically learned to "act white." I stayed in the state hospital for over a year receiving counseling and group therapy. I soon caught on to how the psychiatrists would ask the same question fifteen different ways to see if you would give the same answer. I soon started thinking I was smarter than the doctors. I began to manipulate during counseling, by telling them what they wanted to hear. I was finally released after spending a year in this therapeutic environment and nothing had really changed. I'd been placed on medication, I learned to act white, I learned to manipulate, but internally nothing had changed. I still felt ugly and awkward, unloved and unworthy.

Once I was released back to my grandparents, I started high school. My sister was going out with a guy who introduced me to his brother James. We became high school sweethearts and were inseparable. Once again, I thought I'd found someone who loved me for me. The only thing was that he was not sexually experienced. I was his first kiss, his first girlfriend, and his first sexual experience. I was far more advanced than he. I started playing unnecessary games with him just because he became all emotional over me. I would tell him that I was going to run away from home and that I'd already purchased my bus ticket. He would cry and beg me not to leave him. I would turn my head and laugh at his being so naïve.

One day, I came to school but had gotten off to a late start, so I missed my first period class. James caught up with me at my locker before second period, and asked me why I was late. For reasons I cannot explain, I started pretending I couldn't stand up. I was rolling my eyes in the back of my head like I was about to pass out and started slurring my speech. He immediately grew concerned and I loved it. I lied and told him on the way to school a group of guys accosted me and shot me up with drugs then raped me. This scared him so bad he made me go to the school counselor. Evidently, the counselor knew that I was lying because my story kept changing. That evening I was back in the state hospital once again receiving counseling and medication. I was diagnosed as manic depressive and was treated for another six months. I began to have a hard time separating reality and fantasy.

This time when I got out, James was waiting for me. We went back to school as usual, but I soon found out I was pregnant. I remember when my grandmother took me to the doctor's office. After my examination, the doctor walked out to let me get dressed, and I was alone in the room jumping up and down, silently cheering. All I could think of was that now I'd have two people to love me; James and our baby.

Because of my parent's deaths, I'd always received social security, so my grandparents allowed me to move in with James at the age of sixteen and gave me my social security check to pay my share of the bills. James got a part time job as a bus boy at a local restaurant. We lived together throughout my pregnancy, going to school, and really just playing house. Neither one of us was mature enough to handle living together. We began to fight. Pretty soon our fights began to escalate and became really serious.

James wanted to go to the Air Force. He felt he'd be able to provide better for our family, but I was too insecure for him to leave me for the several weeks of basic training. I think this was the point he began to really resent me. So we would have serious physical fights. The police would sometimes come, but I was never willing to press charges. I would always call my brother to come, pack my belongings and I'd move back to my grandparent's house. This would happen at least once a month. My brother Ernest would get mad about having to come get me and my things. I would get mad that he would never fight James.

Because James was the linebacker on our high school football team, I was no match for him physically. He would often fight me to the point where he would hurt me. Soon I started feeling like this was a part of love. I began to initiate fights, and do things that I knew made him mad so that he would jump on me.

Part of the reason I'd do this is because after each fight, James would feel bad and tell me he'd never do it again. He would tell me how much he loved me, and we would have "make up" sex that was out of this world.

When my daughter was six months old, James and I got into a huge fight and we broke up for good. I was almost seventeen years old and I started dating a guy they called "Steel." Steel and I lived together for a while. What I loved about Steel was that he was a gangster and he would fight anybody. He had guns and a bad temper. One day Steel gave me a ride to James' house to get some money for pampers, and he and James got into it. James felt I disrespected him by bringing another man to his house. I cannot describe the feeling I had when both men were fighting over me. My ego was severely inflated.

A week after this, I received papers served by a constable stating James was taking me to court for custody of our daughter. He was suing me for custody on the grounds of being an unfit mother. Word had got out that Steel had started me to using drugs.

I literally had no idea what to do. I barely glanced at the papers and went about my life, only taking notice of the date I was supposed to appear at court. I knew enough to show up to court. But, I didn't know I was supposed to have a lawyer, and didn't have the slightest clue as to how to go about getting one. As I grew older, this would be another resentment I held towards my family, because no one told me how to defend myself legally in order to keep my daughter.

When we got to court, James' lawyer introduced himself to me and asked where my attorney was. I told him that no attorney had contacted me (thinking that this was how attorneys were obtained) so I did not have one. James' lawyer unethically advised me that I could not talk to the judge without an attorney. So, when the judge gave James a weekend visit with my daughter and reset us for the following Monday, I didn't have a way of getting my daughter back. I didn't have a lawyer, and because of what James' lawyer had advised me, I couldn't mention to the judge that the weekend was over and my daughter had not been returned. Every court date after that was reset because I had no lawyer. No one in my family ever told me how to get one, nor did anyone bother to show up for court with me to see what was happening. Finally, James stopped paying his lawyer and we never went back to court. My daughter never came back from her weekend visit. From that point on James kept her and raised her and would only let me see her when he felt like it.

After I lost my daughter, there was a void inside of me that I could not seem to fill. No drug could fill it up. No man could fill it up.

Before James took my daughter I smoked weed and snorted cocaine occasionally, but afterwards I began hanging with a neighbor in my apartment complex that showed me how to free base cocaine. This was the ultimate high, or so I thought. I began to free base cocaine regularly then I started free basing every day, marveling at my new found freedom without the burden of having a baby.

One day Steel took me to his old neighborhood to visit his old friends. He went into the back room and left me up front. Coincidentally, I had my daughter with me on a visit. I was curious as to why everyone kept going in the back room staying for long periods of time. Inquisitively, I walked in the room and saw that they were all shooting dope. I immediately thought of the time I was thirteen years old being shot up with dope by Regina and how it made me feel. I wanted to shoot some dope.

Steel said no at first, but finally gave in to my pleading. He held my daughter while his friend injected me with a needle full of cocaine. This time, I shot at least twenty five cc's of cocaine. The drug had an even greater effect on me than it did when Regina shot me up. I knew then that I wanted to feel this way all the time. Steel noticing the effect the drugs had on me, started feeling bad about having my daughter in this environment, and strongly suggested we leave.

Soon, I started shooting cocaine daily. My veins were small and often rolled, so I always had to find someone who could "hit" me. I would still get to see my baby occasionally, during these times I could momentarily stop using drugs to spend time with her, but quite often I would miss visits which would enrage James. I was slowly sinking into my addiction deeper and deeper and everyone around me noticed and grew concerned.

My family members had never been confronted with an addiction such as this, so they did not know what to do. I became violent and would often go off on them for mentioning my addiction to me or for trying to help me. I also began to fight Steel. He never wanted to fight me, so he would shake me or grab me and hold me until I would tire of trying to fight him. After I would fight him, I would lie across the bed and cry for hours and scream that I wanted my baby back. When my crying spell would end, I would get up and go get high.

Often, I didn't have money for drugs. So, I began sleeping with a dope dealer on the side who kept me supplied with the cocaine I needed to stay high. Pretty soon, I found out that the dope dealer I was sleeping with was Steel's arch enemy, and was responsible for Steel getting cut up during a fight years before he and I got together. My sleeping with the enemy was causing problems in my relationship with Steel. Although I'd never blatantly disrespected Steel by sleeping with his enemy in our home, I would sleep with him behind Steel's back, and his enemy would always hint to Steel that he was sleeping with me. This would make Steel angry, because he could never prove it.

I became pregnant again. I was using drugs and couldn't stop even though I was expecting. I gave birth to a beautiful baby boy named Eric. I didn't know if the baby was Steel's or his arch enemy. I took my son to my grandparents and asked them to raise him.

Soon my habit became way out of control. Steel, nor his enemy, could keep it fed. One day I met a good looking guy named TBone at a gas station. He had a best friend named Geovonni who was even better looking. They were drug dealing pimps looking for hookers, and I was a hooker on drugs looking for a way to make more money for drugs. They were harassing me about wanting to use the payphone that I refused to get off of. Geovonni asked me what I was looking for. I told him that I was trying to score some dope. He told me that they had what I needed and to come over to their car. When I reached the passenger window, he opened up a briefcase and showed me stacks of money and lots of drugs. I jumped in their car, leaving Steel and our apartment and everything I owned. I never returned.

I started whoring for them. They taught me all about the "pimp/ho" game. Overnight, I became a super star whore. I was an apt pupil, and before you knew it, I was making more money than all their girls. They kept me supplied with as much cocaine as I could do. Just as my habit grew, my lust for the street life grew as well. Not only was Geovonni good looking, he was smart. He started a business front, a company called ABC construction, to sell his drugs. I was the secretary and I loved it. Geovonni taught me a lot, and I also learned a lot from their other hookers. I was so infatuated with him; I would do whatever he wanted. He took good care of me. He never hit me or pressured me when I wasn't making money.

I met a big time cocaine dealer who was an old man. Coincidentally, they called him Old Man Jim. He didn't want me to whore anymore. He wanted me for himself, so I stopped whoring for TBone and Geovonni and moved into my own apartment where Old Man Jim paid all my bills. He kept me with money and cocaine. He was disabled therefore his hands were permanently crooked. He could not chop up the chunks of powder in his cocaine, so everyone came to score from him because his packages were so fat. I would go to his trap and sit there, get high, and just look pretty all day and night. This would go on for days at a time but I soon grew bored with this. I started missing the street life, and the drama of the "ho game". On the cool, I was pimp shopping, hoping to once again meet a good pimp who would put me back out there. One day, Old Man Jim's cocaine connection, Big John, happened to see me sitting in the trap and inquired about me. From what I was told, he came to an understanding with Old Man Jim that I was to be his or he would stop supplying him cocaine.

Big John was a four hundred pound very handsome man. He was very suave and light on his feet and had much class. He was not only a big time cocaine supplier, he was a high-class pimp. He introduced me to a classier style of whoring. The clients were big time con players or men in the game. The tricks were wealthy businessmen, doctors, and lawyers. One of the rules Big John had for all of his girls was to never let a client or trick see you get high. It didn't matter if they knew you got high, you never let them see you use.

It was told to me that Big John used to shoot dope years ago, but had a heart attack and had never shot dope again, but he could "hit" even the smallest veins. I fell in love with him watching him "hit" me and talk to me telling me how good he was going to make me feel. He would tell me how beautiful I was while he would shoot me up with drugs, and I was more or less hypnotized by this. I was Big John's youngest girl and his most requested girl. The drugs would make me freaky and take away any inhibitions I had sexually, and the clients were always extremely satisfied with my talents. One of my greatest talents was giving a man or a woman head. Big John would take me to "ho" out of town, and the whole ride there he would make me suck his penis, so I had plenty of practice. I became orally fixated once I got high and that was what I wanted to do.

A new drug had hit the streets. Crack. Before crack came out, you would buy your own powder cocaine and cook it. When crack first came out, it was called "ready rock." Almost all the needle users were switching to rock. I still hadn't. To me, smoking rock kept you chasing the drug every five minutes. I could function on the needle. Big John allowed me to sell ready rock.

One day a lady named Beatrice invited me to her house to make some sales. Beatrice was the girlfriend of one of my childhood boyfriends named Ron. Ron was the nephew of my former sugar daddy, Old Man Jim. I went over to Beatrice's house, made quite a few sales, paid her and left. A couple of days after this, I went to some abandoned apartments where they sold drugs to score some drugs for myself; and found my little girl sitting on a wet couch in the living room of the crack house. I took my baby and left. Apparently, James' new girlfriend was an undercover crack head. She was in the bathroom with the dope man, and had left my little girl in the living room with other crack addicts.

I was pissed. There was something about seeing my little girl on that couch that made me not want to score any dope that day. Instead, I took her home to my grandmother's house. James was livid. He came to my grandmother's house after he got of work and picked up our daughter. When I told him what happened he was angry and embarrassed and admitted that he knew his girlfriend had a habit, he just didn't know it was that bad.

I went back to Beatrice's house a few days after this to sell more rock. Beatrice and her boyfriend Ron were trying to get me to smoke rock. I refused. I kept telling them if I couldn't wet it and draw it up in a needle, then I didn't want it. On this particular day, no one was buying rock, so I got up to leave. As I was getting ready to walk out the door, Beatrice grabs the back of my hair and tells me whatever money and drugs I have, I'd better give it up. I couldn't believe her and Ron were trying to rob me. I turned around and punched her in the face, and we began to fight. I hit her in the mouth and eye, while she was scratching me and pulling my hair. I over powered her and pushed her down on the couch getting on top of her beating her some more when Ron comes up and hits me from behind. As I turn to fight him, Beatrice runs and gets a knife. She comes back screaming to Ron, "I got a knife!" Ignoring her, I continue to fight with Ron. Beatrice runs up on me and sticks me in the back with her knife. She stabs me five or six times in the back, then takes the knife and stabs me in the throat. I fought for a while longer, but my energy soon faded. I started to lose a lot of blood and everything started going black. I fell to my knees and attempted to crawl out their front door to safety. As I crawled out the door, Beatrice grabbed a pail of bleach water and dashed it in my face. Somehow I got up and walked to the corner store where the store owner called an ambulance.

I woke up 8 hours later from surgery with my family standing over my bed. I couldn't talk. There was a tube in my throat draining fluid from the repair to my trachea. My grandmother stood over my bed and prayed with tears rolling down her face. She kept thanking God I was alive. Even my daughter, who at the time was no more than 2 visited me. She said, "Oh, my poor Mama…."

For the first time I felt remorseful about my lifestyle. My Grandmother was so very upset. I didn't realize how serious my injuries were, and I kept trying to leave the hospital. I was hospitalized for 3 weeks and began to shoot dope in the hospital bathroom. Big John would have someone deliver my dope every few days.

I soon became impatient with the hospital, so I signed myself out against doctor's orders. The nurses and doctors tried to talk me out of leaving, but my habit and my lifestyle was calling me.

I still didn't know why I'd been stabbed. There were several rumors floating around. One rumor was that Old man Jim had me stabbed for leaving him for Big John. After all, Ron was his nephew. The other rumor was that Beatrice was the lover of James' girlfriend and I was stabbed for taking my daughter out of the vacant apartment. I figured the truth was somewhere in between, but it wasn't robbery, because Beatrice and Ron didn't take my dope or my money.

After I got out of the hospital, my drug usage was at around $300 a day - just on the needle. Big John grew tired of my growing habit and began avoiding me. By this time, I'd moved back home with my grandparents and began a pattern of sleeping all day and walking the streets all night turning tricks. I was lucky to have maintained my looks, so I usually caught the high end tricks that spent good money. Always remembering to never let them see me get high, I only used when I was alone. On the streets, it was also best not to let a trick know you got high because they would only pay you score fare.

My aunts started coming by my grandparent's house harassing me about my behavior. There was constant bickering amongst my aunts and I, so I decided to move in with my hustling partner Derrick and started dating a member of the Mexican drug cartel who was known as "Mexican James." Derrick also had a Mexican neighbor named Robert who did drugs as well. One day I was passed out on Derrick's couch, hung over from a night of drinking and drugging, and woke up to Robert having sex with me. I screamed and punched him and made him get up, but he'd already finished ejaculating inside of me. I was scarred from this. I couldn't believe Robert raped me while I was asleep. I was hurt and felt betrayed because we'd become really cool and had spent a lot of time making money together.

A little while after this, Derrick and I started having sex which developed into us having real feelings for each other. Soon, Derrick stopped wanting me to hustle because he couldn't stand the thought of me being with other guys.

So, we became a couple. After a while, I realized I was pregnant. Derrick decided it would be best if we went to stay with his mother, that way I would have regular meals and be in a better environment. Derrick's mother treated me very well. She bought me clothes and clothes for the baby. We were all under the impression that the child I carried was Derrick's. Derrick was aware, however, there was a chance this baby was not his.

When I ended up having a Mexican baby, I wasn't sure who the father was. I loved my baby. He was beautiful. He was a light skinned, curly haired bundle of joy. He had cherub looks. I knew that he was by far the cutest baby I'd ever seen. Derrick promised to raise my son as his own. I even named the baby after him. Living with Derrick's mom didn't last long. We were trying to pass my baby off as being his, but it didn't work, so once again, I ended up back at home with my grandparents.

I couldn't stop getting high and I couldn't leave my baby to go and get high, so I started getting high in my grandparent's home once again. My grandfather, being a preacher, was highly disturbed about this. He and my grandmother would find needles in my drawer or a shoe box I kept under my bed. Sometimes they collected them and put them in a pie pan and burned them. At other times, they would wrap them in drug pamphlets they had got from one resource or another.

I really put my grandparents through a lot of grief at this time. Once again, they were eye witness to the fact that I was slowly killing myself with drugs and alcohol. I was destroying them while destroying myself. My aunts would come out to my grandparent's house to try and get me to leave or to stop using. I would either fight them - or my grandparents, who became my chief enablers, would make them leave me alone.

I thought I was destined to live and die the life of a dope fiend. I would often picture my funeral, where there was nothing nice to say about me, but the eulogy would be a heartfelt warning for others to beware the dangers of drugs.

I thought that I was so strung out on drugs that life couldn't get worse…..but it did.

Chapter 3

ADDICTION

"You are not responsible for being down, but you are responsible for getting up."

-Jesse Jackson

One particular summer day I was hanging out at the neighborhood park smoking weed and drinking beer, talking trash with the fellas when one of the older men asked me if I was William's daughter. I told him that I was so he began to tell me stories about my father and the experiences they'd had. I loved hearing these types of stories, so I was all ears. When he told me that he also knew my mom, I was over joyed. I'd never heard stories about my mom from anyone, so my curiosity was piqued. What he told me turned out to be a horror story. He told me that my mom was literally crazy, and that she'd killed herself. The wind was knocked out of me. I felt like I'd been sucker punched. Although I shook my head in disbelief, this somehow rang true.

I went back home to my grandparents' house, and immediately questioned my grandmother. When I asked her if it was true that my mother killed herself, the look on her face gave me my answer. For the first time ever, my grandmother was at a loss for words. After regaining her composure, she told me that no one knew for sure what had happened, but that my father loved my mother very much and that he cried like a baby at her funeral. At this time, she also told me how my father became estranged from the family.

My father wanted to play in bands and hang out with older guys. One night, he sneaked out of the house to hang with them. When he tried to sneak back in the window, my grandfather was waiting with the razor strap. At the time, my father was sixteen years old. My grandfather whooped my father, so he left and never returned home. My grandmother told me that someone told them that my father was sleeping in an abandoned vehicle. So, my grandfather swallowed his pride and begged my father to come home. But, my father refused.

I cannot explain the feeling that came over me. This added insult to injury and my resentment for my grandfather grew. After this, I became intolerable around the house. I began demanding money for drugs, talking back and disrespecting my grandparents, especially my grandfather. I would even tear up their house when they refused to give me money for drugs. I would leave for days, leaving my baby with them, then come back to the house and sleep for 3 or 4 days and wake up wanting my grandmother to cater to my every need.

I'd met another using addict who had her own place. The only thing was that she had husband and seven kids. Her husband was a using addict as well. I packed up my things along with my baby's belongings and moved in with her and her family. She would give all the kids liquid codeine at night so they'd sleep while the adults got high all night. One evening, she gave my baby a little too much and he was high. His head was rolling and so were his eyes. I got really scared and knew that I did not want my baby living in this environment. So, I went to my grandparents and asked them to take care of this baby as well because I could no longer drag him through the streets and have him at this lady's house. Like the strong, good Christians they were, my grandparents agreed without blinking an eye. I promised them that once I got straight I would come back and get both my children.

As my addiction progressed even further, I started using my children as a means to get money from my grandparents. They had grown attached to them. So, all I had to do was threaten to take them away, and they would search their purses and clothing for any kind of money. My family members were absolutely disgusted with me. They could not believe I was doing this to my grandparents. I really did not realize the harm I was causing others, let alone myself. My feelings were buried under the dope. I was so caught up in my addiction, that nothing, absolutely nothing mattered unless it was a means or a way to get dope.

As my behavior became increasingly worse, so did my tolerance for drugs and alcohol. I was no longer just shooting dope, I started smoking crack. I needed to be high more often on more dope.

I started experiencing hallucinations. I remember being in a motel one night, and I had been getting high all that day on crack, the needle, alcohol, and marijuana. I had a "trick" in the room with me. He paid for a whole day with me, so I sent him on an errand to pick up more booze. As he left, I locked all the safety locks on the motel door and turned around and happened to look down at the floor. There were hundreds and thousands of little black bugs crawling all over the floor. They were crawling up the wall, all over the door, and onto the bed. THEY WERE CRAWLING ALL OVER MY FEET! I was literally paralyzed with fear. I stayed in the same position (my hand on the doorknob) for 2 hours. When my trick returned and knocked on the door, I snapped out of it. The bugs just.... disappeared.

Physically, I was deteriorating. All my life, I'd suffered with a weight problem. In my junior high school years I wore a 9/10 dress size, but in high school, I ballooned to a size 16. It was partially due to the psyche meds I was taking. When on drugs, my weight would plummet. I would wear a size 5/6 or smaller. At this time, I was a 110 lbs. Emotionally, I was dead. I couldn't feel the loss of my daughter or my sons, the worry of my family, nor the issues that were steadily piling up.

Mentally, I was always paranoid and schitzing. I wasn't well and everyone around me knew this. Every time a murder took place or sirens were heard, my family feared it was for me. One girl I'd attended high school with was found murdered on the high school track, and the news put out an emergency bulletin with her description hoping to identify her. I remember my grandmother telling me she received several calls from family and church members, even neighbors wondering if it was me. I was a danger to myself and others, but wasn't able to see it. So, therefore I was unable to ask for help.

As my addiction worsened, the tricks and clients I had became scarce. It was well known by them all at this point that I was strung out and my body was worn out from all the abuse. Pretty soon, I was walking on the highway late nights acting like a damsel in distress hoping the "right" guy would pull over and offer me help. I would get in the car with these men and proposition them and more often than not, they would pay me for a blow job or a "quickie." The highway became my stroll of sorts. No longer was I getting one and two hundred dollar tricks, my rates dwindled to ten and twenty dollars. My hair and clothing were shabby at best, and I became the epitome of a "crack head ho."

Soon, the older men in the neighborhood began passing me around. I remember a group of brothers who took turns with me. They all either sold drugs or did drugs. I started with the brother who sold drugs in the neighborhood. He sold powder cocaine. I would let him have sex with me for hours only for a couple of bags and then go to my neighborhood "doctor." My "doctor" was a man named Jonathan that we called "Sticky." He knew how to hit my small veins. We often shared needles. I also shared needles with other dope fiends in the neighborhood.

One evening Old Man Jim found me and asked if I knew where he could score a couple of ounces of powder cocaine. I knew this was my moment to make a good score and a small comeback. I told him yes and mentally went through my rolodex of connections. I remembered TBone and Geovonni and their small operation. Knowing they would give me a good deal, I called them up and they were willing to give me huge discount on 3 ounces.

As I made the score and drove away to return to Old Man Jim's place, I got pulled over by the police. Jim let one of his guys ride with me to make sure I didn't run off with his money. As the police ran our ID's the guy turns out to be AWOL from the military. I had the ounces sewn in the waistband of my jeans. Once the guy knew the police were going to let me go and take him to jail, he snitched on me. He told the police that I had drugs in my jeans.

I was taken to jail and charged with felony possession with intent to deliver. I'd been to jail before, but never for any long length of time or for anything that serious. I was seventeen years old at the time and therefore tried as an adult. I called everyone I knew for help. My family had never dealt with a criminal case before and did not know how to help me. But, furthermore they were glad that they could sleep at night knowing I was safely behind bars. All the friends I thought I had stopped taking my calls or flat out changed their numbers.

I was frightened and alone and didn't know what to expect. Thankfully, they put me in the dorm with old school women who taught me the ropes. They schooled me on the judicial system, doing time, and surviving in the county jail. One thing a lady named Queenie told me was that whatever amount of time they gave me, I should do it flat and not get out on parole. She said being on parole was like having one foot in prison and the other in the free world. I held that information close to my heart and felt I had the inside scoop on doing time. I actually received ten years of probation. That lasted all of three months before I was back in jail again for a dirty drug screen. My probation was revoked and they offered me ten years in the Texas Department of Corrections. Not knowing that I didn't have to take the first offer, I accepted the ten year prison sentence.

When I got to TDC, I was a like a little frightened girl. Upon arrival, I had an argument with another inmate. We were so loud and combative the argument was deemed as creating a disturbance. We received a major disciplinary case and were classified to maximum security. I was 19 years old at this time. I had no idea what maximum security was. I soon found out that it was where the hardened inmates were housed. Already scared of just being in prison, I was absolutely petrified to live in this cell block.

I was placed in a cell with a woman they called "Big Boom Belinda." My first night in the cell, she placed a list of her own personal rules on the wall. Rules like "no eating after ten," "no flushing the toilet after ten" and so forth. I was so afraid of her that I followed her rules to a "tee." Rumor had it that she was in maximum security for shanking her lover on another unit. She bullied me for the first few weeks of my incarceration. She had a new lover they called "Juicy." Juicy would often come to the cell door when Belinda was away on a pass and harass me. She would tell me to stand up and turn around so she could see my ass, or raise my shirt up so she could see my breasts. I would beg her to get away from the door before Belinda came back.

One day Belinda came back while she was at the cell door. The guards hadn't opened the cell door yet, and Belinda began threatening me. She told me she was going to kick my ass for talking to her lover. I pushed the intercom button frantically begging the responding officer not to open the door because my cell mate was threatening to harm me. The guard asked me what I wanted her to do. I asked to speak to rank.

They secured Belinda in the dayroom and let me out of the cell to go to the command office to talk to the captain. Once in the captain's presence, I did what I was told never to do in prison or on the streets. I snitched. I told the captain that Belinda was bullying me. That she had a list of rules in our cell that I had to follow, and that she was threatening to beat me up because her lover was at our cell door making a pass at me. The captain seemed to understand and said a few consoling words. She said that she would move me out of the cell with Belinda. I was so relieved. I walked back into the cell block with a smile on my face. The guards escorted me into the cell to pack my few belongings, and walked me to my new housing assignment. When I saw the cell they were taking me to I just started crying. They were moving me into the cell with Juicy! That's when I knew that even the prison staff hated snitches.

Belinda then turned her anger on Juicy and told her she'd better refuse housing or there was going to be trouble. Both Belinda and Juicy ended up going to solitary confinement, better known as the "hole" that day. I was finally in a cell with a cool cell mate.

I later hooked up with two other young women from my hometown. Tre' and Shante. Tre' was gay and what they call in prison a "stud broad," because she acted like a guy. Shante' was an Asian girl who talked, walked, and acted like she was Black. We were all seventeen and nineteen years old and started spending our time acting out.

When one of us would act out and go to segregation (solitary confinement), the other two would follow. We were also known as entertainment for the other prisoners because we would rap and dance. We would make raps about doing time, the prisoners, and the guards and the other inmates looked forward to the shows we would have on the recreation field. We would also do crazy things like have food fights and disrespect the officers. The more we would misbehave and catch disciplinary cases, the more good time they would take away from us as a punishment. Tre' and Shante' didn't have as much time as I did, so in the end It was I who ended up doing my time day for day. Meaning, I had no good time. Instead of doing a year and four months in addition to good time and getting out on parole, I did my entire ten year sentence day for day.

When I knew that I would be doing my sentence day for day, I began to fight a lot. I fought the guards and other inmates. Coincidentally, one of the first fights I had was with Big Boom Belinda. I found out that she was just a bunch of talk all along.

During the course of my sentence, I was re-diagnosed as bipolar with schizo-effective disorder and was placed on several different psyche meds. My days were a blur. I was on so many psyche meds that I didn't have a concept of time and each day melted into the next one.

Before becoming incarcerated, the HIV/AIDS virus had just been discovered. At this time the disease was directly related to gay men. But, two years into my sentence, it was discovered that the HIV/AIDS virus was also linked to needle sharing between intravenous drug users. A year later, I heard that all the men I'd shared needles with were dying one after the other from HIV. Shortly after this they began testing in prison, but this was before all the advancements in medical technology made it possible to detect the virus short term. It was told to us that the virus could live dormant in our bodies for ten years and we not even know it.

Before I knew it, I'd reached the ten year mark. I had been abstinent from IV drugs for ten years and I'd done a ten year prison sentence. I was tested again for HIV and tested negative. I know that it was only by the grace of God that I didn't have HIV.

By this time my kids had grown up without me. I literally watched them grow up through pictures. I still couldn't feel that emotionally. For some reason, I seemed to be disconnected with reality. I didn't realize the severity of my actions and how it affected my children.

When I was released, I had absolutely no idea who my kids were. I mean, I knew what they looked like, but I didn't know what they liked or disliked, their fears, or their personalities. I knew I loved them, but outside of that, I knew nothing. I definitely wanted them to respect me. The belief system I grew up with was that they should respect me just because I gave birth to them. I wanted to not only be respected, but be obeyed as well. I didn't understand that they didn't know me as their mother, so they felt they didn't owe me any respect.

For many years, lack of respect would be a source of contention between my children and I.

Determined to put my best foot forward, I stayed clear of narcotics. I still smoked weed and drank alcohol, but called myself "clean" from drugs. I didn't know that weed and alcohol were drugs as well. I felt as long as I didn't smoke crack or shoot cocaine, I wasn't using.

I soon found employment at a local call center doing telephone sales. My natural gift of gab, street smarts, in addition to the proper speaking voice I'd learned from white girls made a winning combination in sales. As a result, I made a lot of money in this position. The fact that I am naturally competitive landed me number one in sales quarterly. I was soon making money that very few top reps made.

I was able to buy a brand new car, lots of clothes and jewelry, and clothes and toys for my kids. I was spending money like it grew on trees. It was short lived though. Too much money for an untreated addict spells disaster. I eventually lapsed into old behavior patterns of missing work, staying out all night, and splurging on material things. This led to me being behind on car payments. Not wanting to lose my brand new shiny car, I decided that selling crack would be the easiest way to make a lot of fast money to catch up on my car note and other bills.

At this time, I hadn't talked to any of my old contacts in years. While searching for them I realized that everyone I shot dope with had died of AIDS. I didn't know a lot of crack smokers, so I began to search for old dealers I knew. I actually found the dope dealer I was having an affair with when I was dating Steel. I wanted to see if he could get me a nice quantity of crack for the amount of money I had. He was able to fill my request.

We rented a motel room and began selling dope from it. The first two days we made a lot of money. On the third day, I woke up to find all my money and drugs gone. I looked out the window and noticed my car was gone as well. Thinking maybe he had gone to hit a lick, I didn't worry too much. Later, the dealer returned with my car and he was high. I was confused. He'd smoked up the crack and spent all the money. He tried to lie by telling me he was robbed, but because I was also a dope fiend, I knew he was high. I was desperate, so I didn't tell him to get lost. Instead, we started again from ground zero. I got a friend to loan me some money and began to flip it into a profit. After a few days of making money he disappeared again. This time he just took off with the money and left the drugs and my car. I said "fuck it" and got high on crack.

What became apparent to me in that moment was that everything had changed during the ten years I was incarcerated. Not only were most of my friends dead, the ones that were once on top of the game were now smoking crack. Crack had become an epidemic. All the pimps I once knew that prided themselves on furs and jewelry were bums on the street, begging for another hit.

I was severely depressed and still didn't have money for my car payment. I went back to St. John's to stay at my grandparent's house once again. My grandmother began fussing at me because the dealership was repeatedly calling her about my late car payments. I began to hide my car at night. I was also on a crack binge.

I'd been up for a number of days when one evening I was stopped at a stop sign and had fallen asleep at the wheel.

The next thing I knew there was a huge crash and my airbags deployed. An older model vehicle made of steel hit me as my car crept into oncoming traffic, and my newer model car, made of fiberglass, crumpled like an accordion. The older vehicle was barely dented. Surprisingly, I wasn't hurt. When the fire trucks and paramedics made it to the scene of the accident, I'd managed to squeeze out the passenger window of my vehicle. They couldn't believe that I was not hurt, or that I'd managed to get out of the car as it was crumpled so badly.

I walked away from the car accident unhurt. My car, however, was totaled. Feeling like a huge failure, I went into a deep depression and an even deeper spiral of drug use. I began to do as I did for so many years…prostitute my body. Selling not only my body, but what was left of my soul as well.

The early sexual violations I experienced as a child were beginning to surface and I began having issues about sex. Drugs helped me to not care about these issues momentarily, but the sexual acts were compiling. I began feeling worthless and dirty. Soon, the drugs weren't lasting long enough to keep the feelings covered. Crack is only a five minute high.

During this time, an influx of illegal, Mexican immigrants were populating Black communities and other impoverished neighborhoods. They became my prime target to trick with. They often carried large sums of money because they didn't have proper legal documentation to get bank accounts. This made them easy marks for robbery as well.

I had an outstanding warrant for my arrest for a marijuana charge that I'd gotten busted for months before. So, I wasn't surprised when police officers showed up at my grandmother's door and took me into custody. I was completely hulled out. I weighed around a hundred pounds, my face and skin was broken out with acne and ulcers, and my hair and nails were brittle. I'd been on binges for weeks at a time, only stopping to get rest when my Nigerian trick would pick me up off the streets to let me eat and sleep at his place for a few days in exchange for sex.

The first week in jail I slept mostly, getting up only to eat. I don't remember much else. The second week I went to the infirmary for the routine battery of tests one takes when being processed into jail. To my chagrin, I was diagnosed as "pregnant."

I couldn't believe it. I struggled to think whose baby it could be. I was prostituting with Mexican immigrants, having sex with my Nigerian cab driver trick, and having casual sex with a hustling partner named "Black." Sadly on any given day and depending on my level of desperation, sex with either of these men would be unprotected. The possibilities of who the father was were endless.

I stayed in jail for four months and was receiving prenatal care paid for by the county. During my fourth month of pregnancy it was discovered that I was having twins. Although I wasn't mentally, physically, or spiritually equipped to handle more kids (couldn't handle the ones I already had), I was excited about the prospect of twins. Twins to me were like some novelty item.

Shortly after finding out I was pregnant with twins, I was released from jail. During my incarceration, I vowed that I would only get high every now and then so that my twins wouldn't be born addicted. I still had no idea of how powerless I was over drugs, and that I was truly an addict. I was convinced I could start and stop at will. I was deeply ensconced in denial.

I was only out for a couple of days when I started back smoking crack. My grandparents were deeply troubled by the fact that I was getting high while I was pregnant. They literally walked around the house crying and praying for me. Watching them watch me destroy myself became unbearable for me. I could no longer enjoy my high. I had to get away from them so that I could get high in peace without the guilty looks.

I moved in with a druggie buddy, Carl, and his dysfunctional family. Their home was completely chaotic. Everyone in the family got high and there was lots of drug traffic, mainly other users who would pay the house to come in and get high. Coincidentally, this was the family of Regina, the dope fiend I used to baby sit for that molested me at the age of thirteen. My life seemed to have come full circle in such a negative way.

While living in this house I started having hallucinating terribly. I felt like they were devil worshipers, and there was an evil presence around me. It got so bad, until it seemed that the whole neighborhood was in on an evil plot.

My hallucinations worsened over time and soon people were aware that I was having them because in the middle of getting high, I would start crying or quoting bible scriptures, even screaming because I'd look up and someone's face would change into a demonic formation. I began to feel everyone had a secret language that I didn't know. All the other dope fiends in the neighborhood seemed to be on one accord, I never fit in. I would often read books while sitting in crack houses, this really wasn't normal to other addicts. None of this stopped me from getting high or from living in this house.

Even when I would stop by to ask my grandparents for money, they seemed to also be a part of the evil madness. I began to feel like my father who died when I was twelve, was really alive and living in their attic. And the whole evil plot was surrounded around keeping his supposed death a secret.

I kept using while I was pregnant, and even prostituted when I could get away with it. Because of my emaciated body, my stomach was relatively small. Although I was six months pregnant with twins, you could hardly tell unless I wore a tight fitting shirt. One night I was turning a trick with three Mexican immigrants and stole one of their wallets. I would have gotten away with it except one of the Mexicans grabbed my purse and ran, breaking the strap off my shoulders thinking the wallet was in it. I didn't have any personal items in the purse, but instead of running away from them, I jumped in the car with them fighting for my purse. The insanity over this ordeal is that the reason I jumped into the car was because I had a brand new crack pipe in my purse.

They finally parked the car a couple of streets away, pulled me out of the car, and commenced to beating me. All I could do was get into the fetal position and protect my stomach. They beat and kicked me for over five minutes until a random car drove down the street.

By the time I made it to Carl's house, I felt like I was having contractions. I wasn't sure if I had peed in my pants, or if my water had broken. Upon arriving at the house the dope fiends that were there were not at all concerned about how I was feeling even after I had told them what happened. All they were concerned with was how much money was in the wallet and how much dope I was going to buy.

Without going to the emergency room or even calling an ambulance, despite the pain I was in, I sat there and smoked up fifteen hundred dollars' worth of crack all night.

I remember being sore for days. I decided to go back to my grandmother's house because I knew she would take care of me. I was laid up for days. My grandmother would rub my back and my legs with bengay. I was craving dope but was too sore to walk and go score it. My babies would not stop moving in my stomach and I knew the reason was because they were addicted as well. No longer able to take their constant movement, I got up and went to go score. I cried the entire way to the dope house. Not just because I was in physical pain, but because I was so tired of hurting my unborn babies. I didn't have enough love for myself to even think about the self-harm.

When I scored, I didn't want to share the dope, so I came home to my grandparents and got high in the back room. I was smoking and crying and praying to God to help me to stop smoking crack for my babies' sake. The very next day, as I was lying across the bed, the police came to my grandparent's house and served me with a warrant for my arrest and took me to jail. I was seven months pregnant with twins and by this time in my pregnancy, I had only gained ten pounds.

I was honestly relieved to be arrested. I truly did not want my babies to be born addicted to crack. By the grace of God, my twins went full term and were five and six pounds at the time of birth which amazed the doctors. My twins were above average weight for twins born to mothers who didn't have a drug problem.

I ended up having to go back to prison. Someone from my family would have to come and get my babies, or else they would become custody of the state.

I called everyone I knew, and no one was willing to help. My grandparents felt they were too old to deal with twins and were already raising two of my children, so they weren't an option. Surprisingly, my sister Yvette, who I really didn't have a relationship with, volunteered to come and pick them up from the hospital and take care of them until I got out of prison.

My twins were truly miracle babies. Not only were the doctors amazed by their birth weights, one of the twins was breach and was born in distress. She was not breathing when they delivered her, but they worked on her and she was able to breathe on her own. I only got to spend three days in the hospital with them. They were so precious. I would smell them and feed them and sing to them. Placing them in my sister's arms and watching her walk away with them was one of the hardest things I ever had to face. The feeling was indescribable. I literally felt like a piece of me was missing.

I suffered immensely with postpartum depression. The nurses let me take one of their blankets back to the jail with me and I would lie in my cell, sniff the blanket and cry for hours.

I was incarcerated for fifteen months. This time, I understood what "good time" was, and I was a model prisoner. I didn't get in any trouble. All I kept thinking was that I had to get home to not only my twins, but all my kids.

While I was incarcerated in Gatesville, Texas, I had unrealistic expectations that my sister would bring the twins to see me every weekend because Killeen and Gatesville were so close. I didn't realize the hectic schedule she had. And, I didn't realize how hard it was for her to work, take care of my twins, and still tend to her own kids and husband.

I wrote a very mean spirited letter telling her she is apparently trying to keep my kids away from me, and threatening that if she didn't come by the next weekend, I wanted my kids to go to the state. My aunt Dorothy got wind of this and wrote me a letter telling me all about myself and how wrong I was. She told me that it was no one's fault that I was a crack head. We were all raised by the same people, and yet I was the only one who had a drug problem.

This is the same aunt who didn't allow me to be the flower girl at her wedding so her letter only added to my resentment. I wrote my aunt Dorothy a letter in response and told her my truths. I expressed to her how mean they were to me while I was growing up in their parent's house. I explained how I had felt all those years, and shared with her how she made me feel at her wedding.

Surprisingly, my aunt felt me. She became my biggest supporter. She told me that she would take care of me financially while I was in prison. She would pay for my prison college courses. Even help me get on my feet once I got out, but if I messed up, she would withdraw her help and be done with me. True to her word, she took care of me throughout my fifteen month prison sentence.

My sister convinced me to parole to her house in Killeen, Texas. I paroled to her and was disappointed with the living situation. Her house was filthy and her kids were unmanageable. When I decided to take my twins and move on my own, my sister and I had a physical fight. She didn't think I was prepared to live on my own, plus she had become attached to the twins. I didn't know how to express myself in words, so I often resorted to physical violence.

I found a nice little four-plex in Killeen. So, I took my babies and attempted to live on my own. My aunt Dorothy came down from Dallas, Texas, and furnished my entire apartment. At this time I was secretly smoking weed and drinking, thinking my aunt would not find out.

Meanwhile, my oldest two sons Derrick and Eric were still being raised by my grandparents. At this time Eric was twelve and Derrick was eleven years old and they were terrors. For years they had watched me terrorize my grandparents, and both seemed to have picked up where I left off. While at the time they weren't doing drugs or anything, they were extremely spoiled and had to have what they wanted when they wanted it. All my aunts started putting pressure on me to get them because they were overwhelming my grandparents who were getting up in age.

By then, I was pregnant by a soldier named Jeremy I met in Killeen-Ft. Hood, Texas. I thought was in love with this man and he convinced me we were going to get married. I fell for this hook, line, and sinker. When I was about to have the baby, he told me that I had too many kids and he just couldn't see marrying me. It hurt me so deeply. I had introduced him to all my friends and family. I was mostly happy because he was someone I could take home. He was the first square boyfriend I ever had. He had no gold teeth or ghetto jewelry. He was just a nice, normal, clean cut guy.

Our relationship became tumultuous. We began fighting physically and cursing each other out. The more we fought, the further he strayed away. Of course, he would return every weekend for sex. Every time he came back, he would talk marriage. I'd let him in and we'd have sex all weekend long. Every Monday morning he was back to telling me he didn't think the "marriage thing" would work.

Emotionally, I wasn't equipped to handle the rejection. I'd never seriously been in love, so I the only way I knew to handle pain was to medicate my feelings with drugs and alcohol. While I was pregnant, I only smoked weed, but I vowed that as soon as I had my baby I was going to smoke crack because I knew it was a major pain killer.

The night I had my son, I called his father to see if he'd come to the hospital with me. He didn't show up until after the baby was born. A co-worker stayed at the hospital with me. I was embarrassed to tell her that the baby's father would not be present, so I told her that he had an emergency at work.

As soon as he came to the hospital and saw the baby, he said, "He looks like me." And, it was the truth. My son was born the splitting image of his father. I thought the baby would make my baby's father change his mind about marriage, but it seemed to push him further away. As soon as I brought my baby home, I began smoking crack again. My baby was only a few months old when I became pregnant again. I had another boy and I named him Michael. This really pushed Jeremy away. He let it be known that he would not be with me any longer.

I smoked freely in Killeen. I didn't have any hallucinations. I didn't feel spooked or paranoid. It was the most freeing time of my using, because I had no one to be accountable to but my children who were not old enough to know any better.

During this time, my family was still pressuring me to get my older sons since they felt I was doing so well. I didn't have the heart to tell them that I'd started back smoking crack. I wanted them to be proud of me, so I went to Austin and brought my twelve and eleven year old sons Eric and Derrick back to Killeen to live with us. I was selfishly thinking I'd have a babysitter so I could go out at night, prostitute and hustle for my drugs and anything else that we needed.

I thought I had everything under control although we were eventually evicted from the four-plex and were relocated to a family shelter. I would be a loving, attentive mother during the day, but at night, I would leave the twins and babies in the care of my older sons and go out and prostitute for drugs and our basic necessities.

I knew with raising children I couldn't smoke crack and take care of them. I didn't know anything about drug treatment or any type of 12-step programs. I didn't know there was help for people like me. So, I did the best I could to slow down on the drugs. The first major move I made towards quitting was getting a job.

I remember the day like it was yesterday. I got hired at the local workforce center to be a janitor. I was so excited that I ran out of the back door to the pay phone that was located at the main house of the shelter which was directly behind our cottage. I wanted to call my aunt Dorothy to let her know that I'd gotten a job and that we were going to be alright after all. My aunt didn't believe I was using drugs, although some of my other aunts were telling her that I was. They were speculating on the vast amount of weight

I'd lost and the fact that I'd been evicted from the four-plex, but my aunt Dorothy trusted me completely.

She was excited when I told her about the job. Ever mindful of my image, I didn't tell her I would be a janitor. She was thinking I would be one of the intake specialists. None the less, she was happy that I was now employed and had hope for my future. I decided to not to go back through my back yard in through the back door. I was so happy that I walked all the way around the corner to the front of my cottage and went through my front door.

As soon as I walked in, a funny feeling came over me. One of the twins, Myla was standing in front of my son Eric who was sitting on the couch. She was crying. My other twin, Myra was sitting on the couch next to him. She looked as if she'd been crying as well. I asked him what was wrong with them and he said that they were just missing me. The twins were pointing at the baby boy Michael who was a year old by now. I noticed Eric sat bent over and did not sit up while we were talking. Something made me ask him to sit back. He started sputtering and I demanded he sit back. He sat back and his penis was outside his unzipped pants.

I felt faint. It was like I was in a dream. I grabbed him by the shirt and asked what the fuck he was doing. He started crying and I started beating him with my fist. I beat him for at least five minutes before I caught myself. I made him zip up his pants but I went and grabbed a knife and told him I would cut his penis off if I ever caught it out again. He was terrified and clearly traumatized, but so was I and so were my other children.

I went into my bedroom to try and calm down. I took the other children with me. The twins could not make complete sentences because they were only two, but Derrick was able to tell me what happened. He told me that he had caught Eric doing it once before but was too afraid to tell me.

When I was calm, I told Eric to come and sit in the kitchen because we needed to talk. I asked him what he was doing when I walked into the house. He explained in explicit detail that he was making my baby boy suck his penis. I kept thinking to myself that he didn't say "lick" or "kiss." This kid was getting his penis sucked.

I tried to listen to him without emotion, but everything in me kept saying...." The devil found you. Your grandparents sent him to live with you...."

He explained that he first started touching him when we were in the four-plex, when I would go out and turn tricks and leave the kids in him and his brother's care. He told me that every night he would tell himself that this would be the last time he did it, but he found himself doing it again and again. What immediately came to my mind was the fact that it was the same thing I'd tell myself about drugs. I knew then that my son had a problem.

I went to work the next day and told my boss what happened. She called child protective services and they came out to investigate. I was completely honest with the investigator. I told her I was a drug user and that I prostituted at night thinking my sons were mature enough to watch the younger kids. I told her that I honestly did not imagine he would be molesting Michael. I didn't even think he knew anything about sex. I had been in a drug induced fog for so many years, I didn't even realized times had changed and kids were coming up faster and more promiscuous than kids in my day.

The social worker suggested counseling for Eric, and made a service plan for the rest of the children.

I could not stop using. I tried, but I couldn't stop. I couldn't even stop using long enough to enroll my son in counseling. Not only did the problem persist, it got much worse.

Chapter 4

Mental Illness

"The only part of our faith in God that is real is what we express in our daily walk. What we believe, we will practice...."

-Ray Geisel

I really don't know how old I was when I started hearing voices. I was probably nine years old when I realized no one else could hear them. I decided not to tell anyone about hearing voices. I was afraid of what would happen; besides, I made a vow when I told my grandmother about my uncle molesting my sister, and her not doing anything about it, that I will never tell "them" anything else. Exactly who "them" was, I didn't know. But I knew that "them" included my grandmother.

For years, I heard a voice that commentated on every move I made, and for that matter every move anyone else made. In the beginning, the voice was mild mannered and cordial but as I grew to have many traumatizing experiences, the voice became rage. The voice would instruct me to fight or destroy.

As I stepped further into my addiction, two other voices joined in. The voices were God and the Devil. I started having incredulous auditory hallucinations. That was the point I couldn't get high in St. Johns anymore. After a while, the voices of God got really bad. They became more demanding. As the voice of God would speak to me, the devil would ask me what he said. As the devil would speak to me, God would ask me what the devil said. They wanted me to choose.

At this time, I wasn't on my psyche meds, only on the street drugs. The voices would sometimes intertwine and I wouldn't be sure if it was God or the devil that I was listening to. The voices had me convinced that the world was coming to an end and the fate of the world depended on my choice.

The devil told me that if I chose him, I could smoke as much crack as I wanted to without repercussions. God told me that if I chose him, he would give me my heart's desires but he would have to kill my father. And, I still thought he was living in my grandparents attic, although in reality he was already deceased.

The voices convinced me that everyone in the world was dead. I was the only living being and that's why I never fit in anywhere. One night I was walking down the side of the highway on my way to score dope with the last five dollars I had. The streets were wet from an earlier mist of rain. I noticed spikes sticking out of the ground on the side of the road with signs on them that said "GAS LINE! HIGHLY EXPLOSIVE!" The atmosphere seemed to change its density. Everything became foggy and the voices of God and the devil barraged me, commanding me to make a choice.

The devil told me that earth was heaven and that's why crack is a gift, and that if I wanted to enjoy a burden free high, I would have to choose him. Then God said if I didn't choose him he would blow up the world and everything in it.

I will never forget the way I felt in that moment. I felt that the weight of the world was literally on my shoulders. I started thinking about my kids and my grandparents; my family members that I loved, all my brothers and sisters and cousins. I even started thinking about the birds and the animals on the earth. Finally, I thought about "ME," and that I didn't want to blow up. So I screamed aloud, "I was taught that Jesus died on the cross for my sins and I'm going to choose God!"

The devil responded, "Fool it that was ME that died on the cross. You had a fake bible. Everyone else's bible is different…"

I'd never been more frightened in my life. I thought I would pass out from sheer terror. I remember running to my grandparent's house going back to my room and getting under the covers with my hands over my ears until I must have fallen asleep.

Now all these auditory hallucinations came up for me when my son molested my younger son. All I could think of was that the devil set it all up to happen. He was going to get me somehow. I was enjoying his crack without committing to him and he wasn't having it.

My mental health was not good. I started not only hearing the voices of God and the devil in my head, but I would turn on the television or radio and they would speak through the actors or news reporters.

I thought when I beat my son Eric it would stop him from molesting my baby. It didn't. Life became really painful for me. I couldn't leave to go and get high because I couldn't trust him with the kids, so I invited a select few people to stop by whenever they wanted to get high. All this time, I was living in the shelter which was a loosely structured environment. I would tell my company to come over when they saw the house manager's lights off.

The few people stopping by were not bringing in enough dope to feed my crack habit, so I asked a neighbor who was also a using drug addict, to watch my kids at night while I went out and turned tricks. I always came back with cigarettes, drugs, alcohol, and plenty of money; paying her cash and drugs for watching them. In my heart, I was doing the best I could to ensure my son was not alone with my kids.

She lived a few houses down. She also had other addicts coming to her house to use as well. Common sense should have told me that I couldn't expect her to do for my kids what I couldn't even do. But, my addiction over ruled any common sense.

One particular night I went about my usual routine of going out to prostitute while she watched the kids. I walked only a couple of blocks when a car pulled over. In it was a white Christian man. He asked me if I lived in the shelter up the road and I told him that I did. He handed me an envelope with one thousand dollars in it and told me he just wanted to be a blessing to someone. I couldn't believe it. I was excited about the money, but my addict mind told me if he was giving me a thousand dollars, then he had more. I tried to talk him into a date, but he refused. When I saw he was sincere about just giving me the money, I took off running back towards the shelter.

I was so happy. I was going to give my neighbor two hundred dollars and keep the rest. When I reached my cottage, the front door was wide open. I walked in and couldn't believe my eyes.

Eric was trying to penetrate Michael.

I understood in that moment how a person can be temporarily insane because that is the only way I can explain the events that took place after that.

I ran to check the other kids. They were in the second bedroom. I stopped in my bedroom as well. I had a box of adult sex toys and pornographic movies and magazines in a box underneath my bed. The materials were so morally filthy to me, that I never even used any of it they were just some things that a trick had purchased for me.

When I pulled the box out I knew immediately that it had been rummaged through. I went through a mental check list of all the things that were in the box and became mortified at the thought of my son seeing the items. Most of the magazines were of hermaphrodites or as the term is known as "chicks with dicks." There were dildos and very graphic porn movies.

I grabbed a dildo and went into the living room where my son had the couch made for bed. I asked him did he know how it feels to get stuck in the butt hole with something. He was crying so hard. And, so was I. I asked him over and over if he knew how it felt. When he finally shook his head no I told him to pull down his pants and bend over. I took the dildo and sexually assaulted him, "THAT'S HOW IT FEELS!"

I was so angry. Never in my life had I felt so angry. I put the other kids to bed and checked Michaels' rectum to make sure he hadn't been penetrated. I stood over my son

Eric that night as he slept. For the first time I started to realize the extreme amount of harm my drug use was causing. I watched my son sleep with his butt cheeks clenched the entire night.

I was horrified about what I'd done. I called my aunt Dorothy in Dallas and told her what my son had done. I then called my grandparents and told them specifically what he'd done. I also told them what I'd done.

My family members began calling CPS making reports. They alleged that my son didn't do it, that it was probably all the tricks I had coming in and out of my house that did it. No one believed me. The initial CPS investigator that investigated the first incident came out to assess the situation. She told me that she had to remove my children from the house.

I remember this like it was yesterday. The date was September 11, 2001-the same day the suicide bombers drove their planes through the Twin Towers. The entire country was in shock and disbelief, and so was I. I couldn't feel a thing for the hundreds of people who were injured or had lost their lives. All I could do was think about my children crying as they got into the case worker's car.

I signed paperwork for my oldest son Eric to be placed in a residential treatment facility. My grandparents came and got him. My family felt that my son was the victim, I the villain, and the baby a casualty of some deranged drug addict trick. As distraught as I was, I could not stop using.

I tried to kill myself using. I wanted to die. I wanted any drug in any amount. I just couldn't face what my life had become.

My sons Darius and Derrick were placed with my brother, my twins with an aunt in Austin. My son Michael was placed in a foster home. I was still in Killeen prostituting with a vengeance. I was doing more drugs than I'd ever done in life. I just did not want to feel. Pretty soon, I was having not only auditory hallucinations but visual ones as well. The devil caught me.

Killeen was no longer a safe place for me. Even though I couldn't stop using, I couldn't stand being away from my kids, so I moved back to Austin and into my Grandparent's home.

I was allowed to visit my kids once a week for one hour at the CPS office. Most of the time I would be late while my kids waited for me. I'd slide in with only fifteen or twenty minutes left in the visit and demand that CPS let me have more time.

I became so irate, that CPS no longer allowed me at the office. They would meet me in a public place, and bring my kids to visit me there.

After going to court, my younger sons were placed with a foster family, my twins placed with an aunt, and my older two sons placed in the home with my grandparents. At the time, I was living in my grandparent's home but CPS had a strong opposition to my sons and I living under the same roof.

My grandmother did something I know was probably the hardest thing she ever had to do. She had to tell me I couldn't live in her home anymore. I cried and cried because it hurt me so bad, but in all actuality, it was the best thing that could have ever happened to me. When I moved out of the home I'd known all my life, I never went back.

I followed my service plan that CPS had for me, and checked myself into treatment. I was amazed. I never knew there was a place that I could go to get off drugs. Because of all the time I'd previously done in prison, I exceled in this structured environment. After successfully completing treatment, CPS told me I had to attend NA or AA meetings. In treatment, I was only exposed to AA, and while it gave me hope that I didn't have to use, I knew that alcohol was not my primary problem.

My caseworker suggested I try NA. The closest NA meeting is the place I still recover at today. My first NA meeting was phenomenal. I loved it. There were people who had experienced some of the same things I had. They were dresed so nicely, and drove such nice cars that I was convinced they had learned to use drugs successfully. After all, how could they have been in the same emotional, physical, and spiritual state such as me and not use anymore? A lot of them were dressed so nice, I figured they were drug dealers. The more I attended meetings and didn't use, the more I began to believe them when they said they were clean from drugs. For the first time in my life, since not being incarcerated, I was clean from drugs and alcohol.

I learned about the disease of addiction from other addicts who suffered with the same disease. During this time, I moved into a residential drug treatment facility for women. This was a six to nine month program. The program setting was a therapeutic community and my first introduction to such. I completed the program successfully. I was so proud of myself. This was the first time I committed to something and followed through.

All this time though, I was mad at my son Eric. I was mad at him because I felt he got my kids taken away from me. I was mad that I had to move away from Killeen; my safe place to use and get high without the paranoia, but, mostly, I was mad at him because I had to stop getting high in order to get my kids back. Through all the milestones I was conquering in recovery, I was still mad at him.

I somehow mentally blocked out what I did to him. I blocked it unintentionally and unconsciously. As I began working the twelve steps, my mind soaked in a lot of the new information. Pretty soon I felt comfortable sharing at meetings and helping newer members.

When I worked steps four and five, my sponsor asked if I'd left anything out. Wanting to do a thorough job for her, I put on my thinking cap. Then all of a sudden I remembered how I'd sexually assaulted my son Eric. I cried until I threw up. My sponsor was trying not to look shocked as I explained to her how the devil sent my son to me just to molest my baby because I was smoking his crack and getting away with it. When I told her how I physically emasculated my son, she cried with me. I had never had anyone share my pain as she had. I never felt I was worth anyone's tears.

The most painful truth that I ever had to hear was told to me when I worked my eighth step. My sponsor told me that ultimately I was responsible for my son molesting my baby. If I had not been in my addiction and out prostituting using a child to baby sit children, my kids would not have been jeopardized. This was a hard truth to swallow. I justified and rationalized that he knew better, and that I didn't even know he was thinking about sex. She followed it up with my lack of parenting him.

When the realization of what I did to my son truly hit me. I was dumbfounded. My son had been trying to seek forgiveness from me and I pushed him away. Now, I realized that it was I who needed forgiveness.

I wanted to make the situation right with my son. My sponsor suggested that I get stabilized on my psyche medication and seek counseling for my son and myself. At this time, I was living in an affordable housing development and had a nice place to stay. I was awarded custody of my son Derrick, Myla and Myra, Darrius and Michael. By this time I had successfully completed all the requirements CPS had in place for me.

I had a call center job that was less than prestigious, but it paid my bills plus it bought me a car. I thought I was well on my way. I was making NA meetings and started accumulating time being clean. At this time, I began dating someone from my job. His name was Mark. I knew little about him. I knew that Mark had a drug problem, but he always came to work so I figured he was one of those addicts who could use socially. Little did I know there is no such thing as a social addict.

Mark moved into my home with my kids and I and for a moment. I thought I was living the American dream. I didn't know my dream would turn into a nightmare.

Upon moving in, Mark vowed not to use drugs. I expressed to him my sincerity to stay clean and work the NA program. I thought he was on board to do the same thing, because he started attending meetings with me, and even secured a sponsor.

A few months after moving in, Mark started acting weird. He would come home late with some excuse and was always "losing" his money. Pretty soon, I caught on. He was secretly smoking crack.

I encouraged him to surrender to the NA way of life, by contacting and using his sponsor and working the 12 steps, but he wouldn't. And, as a result, he could not stay clean. One night, he didn't come home at all. I was calling hospitals and jails to no avail. I was worried out of my mind. In this moment, I could relate to the worry my family must have felt when I was out using.

At around seven o'clock the next morning, Mark walked through the door with some wild and outrageous story. He stank to high heavens and he looked like he had been through the ringer. I made him leave. I'd already packed his clothes and told him he would have to get help from the men at our NA home group because there was nothing I could do for him. He begged for me to let him come in and shower, I still said no. I wanted him to be humiliated when he asked the men for help, that way, he could no longer hide behind his well-kept appearance. I figured that would shock him into getting the help he needed. I also had my kids to think about. I had just won my kids back from CPS and I didn't want anything or anyone to mess that up for me.

Mark moved into his own place and although I missed him, he was seemingly getting the help he needed and we were still seeing each other. I was transitioning from the affordable housing to the next phase of the program which meant I would get a bigger house with more financial responsibility, so I was getting ready to approach him with an offer to move back in when I found out he was messing around with a white woman. All my "less-thans" and insecurities popped up again. I found myself comparing myself to her and wondering how she (who was skinny, old, and unattractive) could steal my man.

I went through a hard time letting go. I physically fought him a few times, and cursed him out a lot of times. But, my sponsor was really working with me on letting go. I didn't know how to get over a man without getting another man, so I started flirting with a new guy at our group named Raymond who had started checking me out.

One day I was having a hard time getting an auto parts store to replace the bum battery they'd sold me, so I figured I'd better take a man with me that way the auto parts store wouldn't keep giving me the run around. I drove to my home group to look for a man who could help me. The only one there was Raymond.

I explained to Raymond what was going on and asked him would he come with me to the auto parts store to see if having a man would make a difference. He got into my car and we drove to the store. When we got to the front door of the store he put his arm around me and said, "I'll just pretend you're my wife." In that moment, I cannot describe the feeling I had. I had never felt that way before. For the first time in my life I felt safe and secure in a man's arms. Not only was Raymond handsome and fine, he was also a sweetheart. What was ironic is that we actually ended up getting married.

Raymond was definitely a charmer. We clicked from the beginning. He was smart, but not in a conventional way. He just knew what to do in any situation. He also made me feel like a woman. If I was stuck on the highway with a flat tire, I would call him and he'd drop whatever he was doing and come to fix it. He was just always coming to my rescue.

Because he was such a charmer, he seemed to always flirt with women wherever we went. At first I didn't feel insecure because at the time, my weight was under control. I weighed maybe 150 and I felt beautiful. He always had a way of making me feel like I was the most beautiful woman in the world.

Pretty soon, I started noticing him not answering his phone when we were together. It was a tale-tell sign of cheating, but I was so caught up in my emotions for him, that I never really made a big deal out of it.

In spite of his inability to be faithful, I wanted to be with him. I had to be with him. A feeling of security was found in his huge arms and I wanted to feel that way forever.

One thing I loved about him is that he was also in recovery and if nothing else, he was serious about being abstinent from drugs and alcohol. I took comfort in that. I didn't want to be with anyone who drank alcohol or got high, because it was too much of a temptation for me.

We went from dating to living together. I soon realized he had some huge defects. One of them was the fact he didn't want to work a regular 9-5 job. He wanted to work for himself so that he could avoid paying all the back pay for child support he owed that accumulated while he was in prison. It was a struggle. At this time, I became used to working, and working hard. I would get these fantastic positions with progressive companies and make really good money.

On top of his defects of character were my own. I didn't realize how low my self-esteem was. I based my worth as a woman on him and the things that he was doing.

All my friends were telling me that he was using me. They said all he did was rode around messing with women while I was hard at work. I finally told him that we couldn't go on like this. Something had to give. I did my best to inspire him and push him to do more, even found really good jobs for him. He would work for a while, and then he would say he hurt his back, collect unemployment or disability, and that would be the end for that job.

He started doing odds and ends jobs for himself, sometimes making good money when he could get a job cutting down trees, but most of the time he would only give me a little something on the bills.

One evening, Raymond told me that he needed to talk to me about something very important. I was scared. I thought he was going to tell me he didn't want to be with me anymore. He told me quite the opposite. He told me that he loved me, but he felt guilty being there helping me take care of my kids when he had a young daughter that was in a bad situation. Her mother had a terminal illness, and his daughter was taking care of her. She wasn't able to be a kid. He wanted to know if his daughter could live with us. I started putting on my shoes; ready to go get her at that very moment.

Eventually, she came to live with us. I didn't think it would be so difficult blending our families, but there was a bunch of sibling rivalry going on. Raymond's daughter, Lakisha, was used to being in the role of an adult, so she didn't like to listen to me when I would correct her. Pretty soon, I started noticing how Raymond would make a difference among the kids. He'd go out and buy Lakisha tennis shoes or an outfit and would not buy my kids anything. He explained that he was just trying to make her feel comfortable, and make up for some of the things he wasn't able to do in the past. While I understood that perfectly, I explained to him how it probably made my children feel. I told him that we needed to come to an agreement that if we couldn't afford to do things for all the kids, then none of the kids would get anything. At that time, I believe

Raymond resented me for saying that and making him compromise on something he wanted to do.

Shortly after Lakisha moved in with us, her mother started getting really sick. I would call her mother and ask if there was anything I could do…if I could give her a ride to the doctor, or bring her a plate of food. Sometimes she would let me bring her food. One of the greatest feelings I had was when she told me that she wouldn't worry about Lakisha when she died, because she knew I was a Christian and that I would take care of her.

A couple of months later Lakisha's mother passed away. Lakisha was very sad and withdrawn. I tried to console her by telling her that she was lucky she had memories of her mom. I explained to her that I lost my mom when I was a baby, so I never knew the sound of her voice or how she looked.

She had a hard time for a couple of month but soon she started feeling better. I would love the memories she shared with me about her mother. Sometimes out of the clear blue sky she would tell me that she was thinking about her mother and would tell me about one of her memories. At those times, I felt close to Lakisha, and I really grew to love her.

Things started getting better around our house. The kids seemed to be getting along better. They would often entertain us by putting on plays. One night they did a reenactment of Cinderella (the ghetto version) and I just about peed my pants. I hate to this day I didn't video tape that.

On the flip side, one of my best friends was getting married. While she was planning her wedding we had a falling out so I wasn't actually in her wedding. But, by the time her wedding day came, we were speaking again, and I definitely wanted to be at her wedding to support her.

Her wedding was small, but beautiful and elegant. It was held in a beautiful church. As I watched her walk down the aisle, I knew I had to get married. It was at that time I started fantasizing about what being married would be like. How it would feel to put on a beautiful gown and have my own special day.

As soon as I got home from the wedding, I told Raymond that I think we should get married, especially since we said when we moved in together that we would eventually tie the knot. He was very hesitant at first. And, this is where my biggest mistake was. I manipulated him into marrying me. I told him that if he didn't want to get married then we couldn't live together. Knowing that he had given up his apartment to move in with me and that he now had his child made things difficult for him. Reluctantly, he agreed to marry me, and we set the date. We went to a pawn shop to get the rings. I wanted to get married so badly, I took the first ring the cashier showed us. It was a really tiny diamond ring that barely fit my finger.

I couldn't wait to show all my friends and family, and tell them that I was going to get married. I immediately began planning my wedding. The entire time I planned it, all I could think of was not being in my aunt's wedding as a little girl and feeling like now I WAS good enough.

Another mistake I made was leaving the church I was with at the time to join the very same church my friend was married at. The church I was with didn't actually have a church building. We met in hotels and rented space at other buildings, because we were so small a group. I wanted the big, fancy wedding and I don't know why I felt like I had to switch churches, but I just felt that the smaller church just wasn't good enough.

The Pastor and his wife at my previous church were baffled as to why I not only got married by the Pastor at the new church, but why I quit their church all together. I still feel guilt and shame regarding that decision. My previous Pastor and wife were good to me. They often helped me when I was short on my bill money or just needed some support.

Nevertheless, caught up in my fantasy, I switched churches and quit taking calls from my ex-Pastor and his wife. I just didn't have an explanation as to why I left, and I couldn't face them.

Raymond and I planned to have all our children in our wedding. Raymond had 2 other children besides Lakisha who lived with their mother. All ten of our children had a part in the wedding. My twins were the flower girls, my baby boy, the ring bearer, Lakisha was my junior bride, and our older children were bridesmaids and groomsmen.

My wedding colors were crème and gold. All my dresses were hand sewn with the exception of my bridal gown. I collected my cake topper and serving accessories from a

Black designer on the internet. Everything was picture perfect.

Two weeks before the wedding, Raymond and I were spending time alone. The kids were in bed asleep and I thought it would be a good time to make love. I began kissing him passionately. Trailing kisses from his mouth to his neck down his throat and chest to his stomach. One of the skills I perfected on the streets was giving head. Raymond would love for me to give him head for hours. As I took him in my mouth, I noticed a funny taste to his manhood. It tasted like a balloon. No, let's keep this real. It tasted like a condom. I've tasted my share, and I know what condoms (latex) taste like.

I was crushed. I wanted to confront him or at least ask him what was going on. I couldn't bring myself to do it. Fear set in. All I could think of is that all my invitations were sent, and the hall and the church were booked. I was scared that if I said anything, he would call the wedding off and I would never be able to face my family and friends. So, I didn't say anything. I kept giving him head as if I didn't know any better.

My wedding day was one of the happiest days of my life. I felt so special, so loved. I felt that I had finally arrived. The wedding went off without a hitch. My favorite part of the wedding was the bell ringers. Raymond's nieces skipped through the church shouting "The bride is coming! The bride is coming!" This took place just before I walked down the aisle, escorted by my grandfather. I felt like a princess. It was like a dream come true. I thought of all the times when I was a little girl how I would wrap towels around my hair like a makeshift veil and pretend to be walking down the aisle.

Our reception was a blast. One of the special moments was when my son Eric asked me to dance. It was sweet and touching. The day could not have been any more perfect.

I wanted to hold on to this feeling forever. Me. The woman who had "too many kids" was an ex-addict and an ex-prostitute was married! Raymond and I rode our pink cloud for a little while, enjoying each other immensely. We soon found a happy balance to our lives. I would work and Raymond would continue to do odd jobs, but he took over the cooking and I took over the cleaning. Because he could cook so well, I noticed that I started gaining weight rapidly. Soon, my hour glass figure turned into the number "8" and I was bursting my clothes at the seams.

The more weight I gained, the more insecure I became. Raymond was still his normal, flirtatious self, but I became increasingly aware of the way other women would react to his attention. Soon, I started confronting him about the behavior. He was angry about it. He felt as if I were trying to control, change, and "henpeck" him. I would often share with my sponsor how I felt and she would tell me how to say what I needed to say to him in a healthy way. I explained to him that my insecurities were not about him- they were about "me," and how I feel with the weight gain.

I asked Raymond if he could help me get through this rough period by not flirting as much with other women and showing me more attention. I thought he "heard" me. The problem seemed to progress and pretty soon we began arguing. The more we argued, the more he found it necessary to leave the house and get some space from me. During these times, my mind would race with all the horrible possibilities of what he could be doing and who he could be doing it with. I began suspecting the women in my NA home group of flirting with and trying to sleep with my man. It seemed the more I shared about my feelings of insecurities in meetings, the shorter their skirts got.

Pretty soon, I began eating more and more, finding solace in food. I would eat until I was stuffed. I wanted rich, starchy, fattening foods. I think they call it comfort food. It would make me feel somewhat better while I was eating, but soon after, I would hang my head in disgust. I would feel sick, sad, and sorry like I had smoked a pound of dope. My weight ballooned to 415 lbs. I began noticing every time my husband looked at another woman. Even if my husband and I were not together, I would look at women and think, "He would like her," or "He would want to have sex with her."

I would compare myself to other women and would always feel less than. I began to hate myself. I think in some ways Raymond tried to help me. He started cooking lighter meals and used non-fat cooking spray instead of cooking oils, but nothing helped. I felt I was too far gone. I would exercise for a week at the most and when I didn't see any results, I would quit. He became exasperated with me. Not knowing what to say or how to say it without hurting my feelings. All I wanted was for him to reassure me that I was still beautiful and attractive to him, that he loved me, and that he wasn't going to leave me. One of the most insane things

I did during this time was trying to wear my old clothing that no longer fit. I was used to dressing sexy, but conservative. I wanted my husband to look at me the way he looked at other women. That wasn't working out. He would get really frustrated and angry every time I put on something too small. Instead of lovingly telling me that what I had on was inappropriate, he would fuss at me and say things like, "I can see your stomach!"

Because of the twins, my stomach was stretched. Coincidentally it is the first place I gain weight, so it often overlapped my pants or hung below my blouses. I felt desperate. I felt that at any minute my husband was going to tell me it was over because I no longer looked the way I did when we met. I lived in constant fear. I would tense up every time a beautiful woman walked in the room, and if she was pretty with a nice shape, I'd get a sinking feeling right in the pit of my stomach.

Raymond was still hustling during the day. He often made money moving people's furniture on his old beat up truck. All of a sudden, I started noticing that most of his customers were women. I became very apprehensive about this, imagining him going to some woman's house or apartment to move her, and her coming to the door in lingerie.

Pretty soon, my jealousies and insecurities took a turn for the worse. I began announcing in NA meetings that I wanted the women at our group to stop calling my husband asking him to move their furniture or repair things at their house. The women at my group thought I was losing it, and

I was. I made this announcement each time I shared in every meeting I attended.

During this time I would often find numbers in the pockets of his pants or in his car. One day, I found condoms in his car and had a fit! I questioned, interrogated, threatened, and accused him of everything my mind conceived him to be doing. He told me that he was holding them for a friend of his who was married and was cheating on his wife. That was it. I knew I was going to lose him. I began to fantasize about getting high again, losing the weight instantly. At this time, I had almost five years of sobriety, and I figured I could get high just long enough to lose the weight, and then go back to not using.

Raymond and I would often argue about my not wanting him to move the women at the group. Again, he thought I was trying to control him. Truth was, I didn't trust him or the women. When we would argue, it would feel as if my world was coming apart. I was often scared to defend my point figuring he would use that as an excuse to walk out on me. I began having really bad temper tantrums. Crying for hours at the slightest remark he made that hurt my feelings. He didn't know how to help me. I didn't know how to help myself. I began threatening him with drug use. I would tell him if he did or didn't do certain things I would use. For a while, it worked. He started spending more time at home and less moving the women at the group, so I started feeling a little better about myself and our situation.

My friend whose wedding I attended shortly before Raymond and I were married purchased a new house. She was living the life I wanted to live. Doing all the things I wanted to do. I started applying for home owner loans. It wasn't that my credit was bad; I just didn't have any credit. No mortgage company would give me a loan at that time. My credit score was just too low. They would offer me advice on how to build credit by getting secured loans and credit cards, but as it was, I was living pay check to pay check, not really having the available cash to put towards a secured loan or card. So, that wasn't an option for me.

Soon I started looking for leasing specials. I was hoping I could get something that was "rent-to-own." I found a realtor who was willing to work with me. When I showed Raymond the house online, he was ecstatic. He was treating me like I walked on water. Really wanting to please him, I moved from the affordable housing program we lived in to paying rent that was twice as much.

The house was huge. It was a two-story, five bedroom home, big enough for us and all of our children. Everyone was excited and happy for us. The only problem was that Raymond had a thirty thousand dollar judgment on his credit for back child support accumulated while he was in prison. The realtor worked with us anyway, putting her job at risk by falsifying some documents. I didn't realize I was going about things the wrong way. I still had a "street life" mentality, and didn't see anything wrong with the Black realtor "hooking her sista up!" So, against my better judgment, we moved into our expensive, new home.

We threw a huge barbeque inviting our friends and family. Raymond's family came. They kept saying how proud they were of us. I couldn't get enough accolades. I began lying to everyone telling them that the house was "rent to own" when in all actuality, it was a simple lease. I wanted all my friends to think that I was doing the same things they were; buying houses, getting married, and living the American dream.

I started getting fearful. I often lied to Raymond about how much money I made. I would come home from work and tell him wonderful news about how I'd gotten a raise or a promotion. In my mind, I was solidifying our relationship. I wanted to keep him by any means necessary. What I soon realized was that those lies were adding up. Not only were we living beyond our means in the new house, Raymond was depending on me more and more. Because of the weight, I was often lazy and lethargic, neglecting house work. He would often complain about my lack of cleaning the house and washing clothes. It all seemed to be too much. I was getting overwhelmed.

One thing I was happy about though was the relief he brought with my children. I loved it when they asked me for something and I would say the words, "Go ask your Daddy." My children called him Daddy and even though we were struggling financially, I'd never been happier. I was also still having insecurities. I even knew he was cheating on me at one point, but I decided to ignore it for the sake of keeping face among my family and friends. Raymond and I were still on shaky ground.

We decided to take an NA road trip and go to a nearby city to attend an NA convention. We were already low on money, so we decided to share a room with fellow lesbian members Lisa and Melanie. Melanie was very popular at our group, especially among men. She wasn't all that pretty, but she had a body that wouldn't quit. She had a perfect shape with a nice butt to boot. I was hesitant about sharing the room with them, because I knew that although Melanie was in a lesbian relationship, she also "did" men.

It was worse than I imagined. During our weekend, Melanie sported ultra-tight, short, outfits that accentuated her body. It seemed that every time she changed, she wore something tighter and more revealing. I felt frumpier and frumpier as her outfits changed. I would look at my husband out of the corner of my eye to see if I could catch him looking at her, and I did catch him a couple of times. There was that feeling again. The feeling that I would get in the pit of my stomach that would make me feel as if he was going to leave me for this woman with the "banging" body.

Needless to say, I was miserable the entire weekend. Ever so good at putting on a mask, I acted as if I enjoyed myself. I walked with confidence even though I felt like a beached whale. When the convention ended we checked out of the hotel and walked through the parking lot with Melanie and Lisa to put our bags in our perspective cars. Melanie and Lisa were walking behind us holding hands and we were walking in front holding hands. I was relieved that the weekend was over and I could get my man away from this vixen. While we were walking, Melanie pulled Lisa and hurried in front of us telling us that we were walking too slowly. I was livid. Only another woman would understand the move Melanie made. I knew as sure as day that she hurried to walk in front of us so Raymond could watch her ass sway. I watched him the entire time out of my peripheral as he tried not to look at her ass.

When we were finally on the road to come home, I began to cry. Raymond let out a deep breath as if to say "What's wrong now?" I tearfully explained to him how I felt the entire weekend with Melanie dressing so provocatively. I asked him if he liked her, did he want to have sex with her, if he was looking at her, if she was naked and I was dead would he screw her? I tearfully grilled him all the way home until he just couldn't take it anymore. He screamed that she was gay and he didn't look at her like that. It only infuriated me more, because I knew for a fact that no one gave a flying fuck if she was gay. All the men at the group wanted to "do" her. He begged me to just leave the subject alone. He didn't want to discuss it anymore. I left it alone, but I never forgot how I felt that weekend.

After getting home and getting back into the groove of everyday living, everything was going along fine until one day I went to our NA group and walked up on him talking to Melanie. I didn't think anything of it at first, but they both had guilty looks on their face. I soon became suspicious. When we made it home that evening, he approached me and told me that Melanie asked him could he move her living room couch to her new apartment, because she was breaking off her lesbian relationship with Lisa and was moving in with a man. He tentatively asked me would it be alright if he did it. "Absolutely not," I said without a thought. He became incensed and asked me why he couldn't. I told him because this proves she's not gay, and she may come to the door in her panties. We argued like never before. He was fuming, and it enraged me.

Why was he putting up such a fight? Although we'd had several discussions about him moving the women at our group, he never felt so adamant about being able to move whom he wanted. We argued. I cried. He fussed. I screamed. Finally, he conceded. He told me that if it bothered me THAT much, then he wouldn't do it. We went to bed and for the first time since we'd been together, he didn't hold me while we slept. I was torn up on the inside.

I called my sponsor and spelled out the entire story. She already knew how I felt the weekend of the convention sharing a room with Melanie and her lover, so she told me she understood where I was given the fact that my self-esteem was so low. She suggested I called Melanie and talk to her woman to woman and explain how I felt. So, I followed her suggestion. I called Melanie and totally took ownership of my insecurities due to my weight gain. I asked her if she could please find someone else to move her couch until I can get in a better place emotionally. I explained that it was nothing personal, that I felt like that towards all women at the group. She told me she understood and that she would definitely get someone else to move her. I felt good. I felt like for the first time, I owned my feelings. I called another woman and allowed myself to be vulnerable, open, and honest with her, in spite of my fears.

Raymond was still acting angry. For the next couple of days he hardly spoke to me or touched me. I called my sponsor again to ask her was I wrong for the way I felt and for how I handled things. My sponsor told me that this is the part of sponsorship that's hard. Confused, I asked her what she meant by that. Lisa, who is Melanie's ex-lover, was my sponsee-sister, meaning we shared the same sponsor. My sponsor goes on to tell me that Lisa called her the night that Melanie moved out and told her that Raymond was moving Melanie's couch. When Raymond realized Lisa was talking to our sponsor he begged them both not to tell me. He also swore Melanie to secrecy.

Words cannot express how I felt at that moment. All I could think of is that Raymond and I made a decision as husband and wife and all it took was for some floozy to bat her eyes at him, and he totally went against me for her. Then the fact that everybody knew except me, was a betrayal within itself.

I was outraged. I couldn't believe that my husband would allow another woman to make me feel like I was nothing compared to her. It once again took me back to my old ho mentality...."Another woman got one up on me."

As soon as Raymond walked in the door, I jumped him. I kicked and bit and scratched and hit him with my fist. He had never seen this side of me. He begged me to let him explain, but I wasn't hearing it. Nothing I'd ever been through in life hurt me as much as this did. To this day, I cannot explain why it hurt so. I was mad. Raymond finally held me down long enough to talk to me, but I wasn't listening to anything he said. All I could think about is how I opened myself up to him, to Melanie, and how they both shitted on me.

Friday nights at our NA group are like going to a night club. Every one dresses up and people come to "share" their asses off. This Friday was going to be different. I was going to confront Melanie and I didn't care who was around or who heard.

I sat through the meeting rocking and staring at her. Everyone could feel the tension. A lot of the members had heard through the NA grapevine what had happened, but no one expected me to do what I did. Little did they know my tape was playing loudly in my head. "You're not good enough...and everyone knows it." Before the meeting actually ended, I saw Melanie go to the restroom. I was waiting outside the door when she came out. I told her that she needed to pay my husband whatever she owed him, but as long as she lived she better not let me see her ever speak to him or me again. She started working her neck and was about to say something sarcastic when I hauled off and punched her in the face. I grabbed her by her hair and was about to punch her again when a lot of the other women jumped on top of me and held me on the ground. Raymond runs in and starts pulling them off of me telling them to get off of his wife. He is frantic at this point. Again, he'd never seen me like this. He began apologizing profusely, telling me this was all his fault and that he was wrong, but to please just stop. They finally got us separated. One of her friends called the police. The officers took statements from both of us. Two weeks later, both Melanie and I had relapsed.

Giving up my clean date was the hardest thing in the world to do. I was so hurt and devastated about the betrayal by

Raymond that I just wanted something to ease the pain. I wanted to lose the weight so that he would find me attractive again, and I wouldn't have to be jealous of any other woman. I wanted to run from the surmounting bills that were accumulating from living in a house we actually couldn't afford, but most importantly, I wanted to pay him back. I wanted to hurt him like he'd hurt me, and I couldn't think of a better way to do it.

At first, I kept my using a secret. I would go to work early and score drugs before going into work, leaving them in my car until I got off, and smoke crack all the way home. I would get in from work and would have no appetite. I just wanted to have sex with Raymond to enhance the feeling of euphoria that I felt from getting high. I even had to be careful with that. Raymond and I had a set sexual pattern and any kinky deviation would cause suspicion.

Pretty soon, my using progressed. It was getting harder and harder to maintain my secret. One night as Raymond slept, I went out to score some crack. When I got back, I couldn't believe he didn't even notice I was gone. This added to the disillusion that I was actually getting away with getting high. I sat on our back patio and smoked while Raymond and the kids lay fast asleep in bed. All I could think of is how once again, I used when things got too rough for me.

I picked up my cell phone and from the backyard patio, I called Raymond who was still upstairs asleep. He answered the phone sleepily, and it took a minute for him to be coherent enough to understand what I was saying. I told him that I was downstairs on the patio getting high on crack and for him to please not come down. He kept asking me was I serious. I told him yes I was. For the first time since we'd been together, my husband cried like a baby. Part of me felt bad, but there was a part of me thinking I hope it hurts him like he's hurt me.

I finally came upstairs. He was wide awake, talking to his sponsor on the phone. He told me to give him my bank card and my credit card. I did, but I had already spent most of the money. He was devastated. How were we supposed to pay our rent? I couldn't think of anything. We talked for a little while, but he just kept crying asking me what happened. I told him that I'd been getting high for the last two weeks that I was so depressed and hurt that I couldn't make it through all that clean. I told him that I didn't want to talk anymore. I told him that I had a little more crack that I wanted to finish downstairs. He looked at me as if he didn't know who I was, as if I were a stranger. Here I'd gone from someone who was eating, breathing, and sleeping the Narcotics Anonymous program, to someone who was clearly high and insane. It took an hour to finish smoking. When I came back upstairs, Raymond grabbed me and threw me on the bed and made love to me like never before. It started becoming a ritual. I would get high in the evenings and he would make love to me all night. It was almost as if he were getting high off me.

Very soon I started running off for days getting high, leaving him with the kids. He would come and look for me. Sometimes he found me and would make me come home, other times I would be watching him from the window of a crack house as he rode up and down the street trying to catch a glimpse of me. Once, I rented my car to a drug dealer and he wouldn't return it. So, I called Raymond. He came up on the streets and forced the drug dealer to get out of my car, and then threatened him that if he ever took my car again, he would beat him up.

As always, my using got out of hand. My kids were looking at me baffled and confused, not used to seeing their mom like this. I was out of my mind. All I wanted to do was use drugs until the pain went away, but the pain only seemed to get worse. Raymond tried to stop me from using. He would take my battery out of my car so that I couldn't leave. He would also beg, bribe, and threaten me. However, I couldn't stop.

Someone called CPS. I was devastated, but not devastated enough to stop using. I took it for granted that now that I was married, Raymond would automatically see to it that I didn't lose the children. The CPS caseworker stated that I couldn't be alone with the children and the only way they could remain in the home is if Raymond committed to staying there with them. He told CPS that he couldn't take care of the kids alone. So he took his daughter and moved out. My kids went to a shelter. That added insult to injury. Even though I was using and making terrible decisions, I never thought for a moment that my husband would leave me and not take care of my kids. All I kept thinking was that I took care of his kid **and** her mother!

The night before Raymond moved out, he cooked a special dinner and also took our wedding cake we'd traditionally saved out of the freezer. It was one year ago that we were married. It was our anniversary, and I had forgotten in my drug induced haze. I came in about midnight. The dinner was cold and Raymond was colder.

Once Raymond moved out and the kids were gone, I attempted to continue to work and stay in the house, but everything was falling apart. I couldn't stop using. I started using in the parking lot at work, coming in from break sweating and looking bug eyed. It became apparent to my coworkers and supervisor that something was terribly wrong. One day I had fallen asleep at my desk after being up on a binge for days. My supervisor called me in her office where her direct supervisor and the HR worker were having a meeting about me. I was going in and out of consciousness. One moment I would be wide awake, and the next in a deep sleep. All I remember is waking up as I was telling her how I'd relapsed over my husband cheating on me. I was mortified when I realized I said those words out loud and to my boss. She asked me was I high right now, and I truthfully told her that I had been getting high nonstop, also getting high in the parking lot. They fired me on the spot. I was even more depressed.

I kept getting jacked on the streets by drug dealers and dope fiends. They were selling me fake dope, running off with my money, and just over all giving me a hard time. They were wondering what kind of dope fiend drives a new car and that got her hair and nails done. By then, a woman who I'd been in prison with named Elise hooked up with me on the streets. She started protecting me from the dealers and dope fiends, and then she just moved in my house. She would run off in my car, leaving me stranded often. But, she would always show back up with money and drugs. She was my only friend at the time, and she was all I had.

I stopped going upstairs in my house, living only in the spare room I used as an office in earlier times. The upstairs bedrooms still had the scent of my children and it would literally kill me to walk up the stairs and smell them. My computer was still in the spare room and the internet was still connected. I was running out of options and ideas. I'd used all my savings and my credit cards and had gotten several pay day loans. I started writing checks with Elise and that would get us up to 400 dollars at a time. I thought I was managing the addiction, but soon, we'd burned up all the banks. Too scared to whore on the streets for fear that Raymond would catch me, I turned to the internet.

I started placing ads on a personal website with illicit pictures advertising as a dominatrix. All I wanted to date were white guys. I learned a long time ago in my past as a street hooker that black men didn't make good tricks. I started investing in my new profession, buying leather lingerie, whips, toys, and chains. I charged three hundred dollars for an hour session. During this time nine hundred dollars was a bad day. I would usually make around twelve hundred dollars on a good day. I started getting scared of Elise, thinking she would have someone rob me, so I started calling Raymond asking if he could come on the streets and pick up my money. Of course, I would have to give him some of it. He asked where I was getting the money and I told him that I was giving massages.

So many rumors were running around. People were telling my husband that I was prostituting on the streets, jumping into cars with his friends, but that was untrue. I received my last paycheck in the mail and was going to spend it all on drugs. By a fluke, my husband ended up getting to the mail before I did. He refused to give me my check. We argued over the phone, hanging up in each other's faces, then calling back, and hanging up again. He didn't think I needed to have my check, he said we still had bills left over to pay. Finally I told him to keep the check. I knew I had a trick coming over so I wasn't worried about the check. When I told him I didn't want it, he became suspicious and decided to drive out to our house.

By the time he made it, I was inside turning a trick. The trick was an older white man who couldn't even get an erection so all he was doing was rubbing on my body. Just then, the door swings open and Raymond is standing there looking furious. I had forgotten to lock the top lock on the door, so Raymond was able to open the door with his key.

He beat the poor old white man senseless, breaking his own hand in the process and making the man leave out of our house naked. I screamed, grabbed my money off the coffee table, and ran upstairs. Raymond followed. I locked myself in our bedroom with him pounding on the door yelling at me to open it. I refused. I kept telling him that he was scaring me and I thought he was going to hurt me. He calmed down a little and promised he wouldn't.

When he finally got me to open the door, he just kept asking how I could do something like this. I didn't have any answers, but I just kept relishing the fact that he could now see how it feels. He refused to give me my check so I grabbed his cell phone and said, "Well let's see who it is you've been occupying your time with." He immediately gave me the check. It just confirmed my suspicions. He wasn't lying around hurting and feeling sad for his infidelities. So, he still wanted to play...... I wasn't through either.

I had heard that my husband was sleeping with another woman at our NA group. This made me crazy. It was bad enough he was sleeping around to begin with, but it felt like a slap in the face for him to carry on with someone at our group, the only place I had to recover.

I confronted him several times. When I would stay clean for a day or two, I'd go to the NA meeting and pick up a white key tag in hopes of trying to get back into the recovery process. The woman would come up to Raymond and make a joke or often say something to him almost as if she were mocking me. This would further enrage me and I would just go back out and use some more. What hurt the most is that I would mention to Raymond that this is what she was doing, telling him to put a stop to it, but he seemed to be drawn into her game. It became apparent to me that he was keeping score. It was his turn to hurt me.

A couple of weeks later, I had called Raymond and told him that I was tired of using and hurting myself, that I wanted to go to treatment and I needed his help. I knew he still loved me and he had hope for me. He drove up on the street and found me crying. He pulled over and asked me what was wrong. I told him that I had three dollars and with all the money I had spent on the streets, no one would sell me any dope. Again, he looked at me like a stranger. I'm sure he was wondering how his wife could belittle herself begging for three dollars worth of dope.

He kept trying to coax me into the car, but I wouldn't get in. I wanted some crack. Finally, he said he'd buy me a dime rock if I just got in the car. He bought the dope, and I relented and got in the car. I believe that was a major turning point in our relationship. I saw the pain in his face as he gave me the dope. I saw the hurt in his eyes as I rushed in the bathroom as soon as I got home.

After I finished, he knocked on the bathroom door and asked me would I go to treatment. I told him the only way I'd go to treatment is if he bought me some more dope. We argued about this. Finally, the dam broke. I broke down and cried with everything in me. I cried for everything I had loss, for the heartache I'd caused my kids, for losing my clean date, and for losing me.

I told him how much he hurt me when he betrayed me with Melanie. I was crying so hard I could hardly get the words out, explaining exactly how it made me feel. I think it was then that he realized how much the incident truly affected me. He sat down on the floor with me and grabbed my hands and looked me in my eyes. He asked me if I could just forgive him for the past, if I could just forget about all the cheating and the lies, if we could just start all over from this point. Because I wasn't ready to stop getting high, I looked him in his eyes and said "no."

I've always wondered what would have happened if I had said yes. What would life have looked like after that point? At the time, I couldn't think that far. I just know that I wanted to be higher and higher and higher, not ever feeling anything again.

Eventually, I went to treatment, but thought after a week I thought I was cured, so I signed my self out. I didn't understand that once I released the addiction again, it would be hard to stop using. It got progressively worse.

I received an eviction notice to vacate the house. I couldn't stop using long enough to get all my furniture out. I had some really nice furniture that I had bought with my previous year's income tax. For four months after I was told to vacate the premises, I was still living in the house. The electricity was off. There was no running water. And, the floor of the one room I lived out of was littered with broken glass from the many crack pipes I'd smoked off of.

Finally, I received notice that they were going to forcefully remove me from the property. Raymond took some pity and decided to help me get as much of my belongings out as he could. He was shocked to see the animalistic conditions under which I was living. The last meal he cooked before moving out was still on the stove full of maggots. The toilets were filled with feces and the smell was horrid. He moved what he could to my best friend's garage and the rest was left in the house. We still had wedding gifts that hadn't been opened that were left behind.

He brought his older son to help move the furniture and he told me that he was ashamed to even let him see what I had done to the house and to myself. I was ashamed as well. From that point on, I was no longer using to hurt Raymond.

I wasn't even using to get high. I was using to punish myself.

After much using, I had no other choice but to check into treatment. I went to jail for sleeping in an abandoned building and when I got out of jail, I realized I had nowhere to go. A lady from the AA fellowship took me in and allowed me to sleep in her spare bedroom until a bed became available for me in rehab.

Once I was clean, it really hit me how much I'd messed up. My poor children were in foster care. I would visit them from time to time, but not as often as I could have or should have. Once I got to rehab, they became my number one concern. The counselors at the rehab tried to get me to see that my children should be the last thing on my mind. My first order of business was to focus on getting clean and staying clean.

I was determined to stay clean so that I could get my children back. I decided to put my best foot forward and throw myself into the recovery process. I participated in all the classes and discussions, talked honestly and candidly to the counselors, and just gave my every effort to appear "recovered." When I successfully completed the 28 day program, I stayed in a sober house, got a job, and soon thereafter a vehicle. I was making preparation to get my kids back, so I worked very hard to get these things back in order.

I talked to a manager of an apartment complex, telling her my story. I told her that I was fighting to get my kids back, and that I was a recovering addict. Because she was also a recovering addict, she fought her superiors for me to get into one of the apartments.

I checked off the list of services CPS asked me to do. Passed every drug test they provided. I also had my supervisor at work write a letter of character reference for me, explaining that I was an exemplary employee, outstanding in sales and leadership.

The judge was impressed and for the second time, awarded me custody of my children. We moved into our new apartment. It was only two bedrooms, so Myla and Myra who were eight at the time, balked at having to share a room with their little brothers Darius and Michael. They were also disappointed at not having a lot of space to play like they had at our "big house." I tried to make it seem like such fun, telling them that we had a lot of neighbors with kids to play with, but they were still not as happy as they were previously.

During this time, I was still having sex with Raymond. Legally we were still married, so I still considered him to be my husband and I his wife. I always felt that our separation would eventually end, and we'd go back to being husband and wife.

While I was using, one of my group members took the illicit pictures off my ad that I had placed on the personal's website, and showed them to other men at our group. Raymond never got over that. But, he kept leading me to believe that eventually we'd get back together. He would always come and help me whenever I had a problem with my car or needed something fixed, but he always asked me for money.

Again, my friend would tell me that he was using me. They kept telling me that I needed to get my divorce and be done with the marriage because it was over. Every time I would bring up divorce to Raymond, he would tell me that he didn't want a divorce, he just wasn't ready to move back in together yet. Little did I know, he just wanted all the benefits of marriage, he just didn't want the commitment.

I was hurting again. I was happy that I had my kids back, but I was so overwhelmed with it all. I made enough money to pay my rent, but there were also school clothes to buy. Darius' father provided minimal child support, and because I didn't know who the twins' father was, everything was all on me. I wanted my husband to come back to me and for things to go back to the way they were.

Once again, I found myself about to use. I knew I had to quit sleeping with Raymond. My sexual issues were tied into my using and the sex with him was becoming an issue. I kept using sex as a way to get him back, but it just didn't seem to be working. I thought because he couldn't stop sleeping with me that meant eventually he would come back to me. What I didn't know is that he was just taking what I was giving.

One of the team leads at my job, Matthew, was making passes at me. I was very uncomfortable with this because not only was he married, I was friends with both he and his wife Julia. His wife worked off and on at our company. I would often confide in her about my failed marriage and how it hurt so bad that my husband and I were no longer together.

I had never been pursued by any man like Matthew pursued me. He bought me anything and everything I wanted, even without me having to ask. His wife Julia took a leave of absence from our job and he really began hounding me for a date. Because I was so vulnerable and felt so bad about myself, the attention gave me a heady feeling. I decided to sleep with Matthew. I wasn't even attracted to him in that way, it was basically a way to get over Raymond.

All it took was for me to have one sexual encounter with Matthew and it was over. He was hooked. He left Julia and moved in with me. Around the same time, my older son Derrick was in a major car accident and broke his neck, so he also had to move in with me, bringing his girlfriend Diamond who was a stripper. At this time, there were eight people living in my two bedroom apartment.

Julia was crushed. She couldn't believe that I would hurt her that way. She just kept saying over and over how she was there for me as I cried over my husband, and that she couldn't believe I was going to hurt her by sleeping with her husband. My sudden need to get what I wanted when I wanted it, would not allow me to feel guilty. I told her that I was in love with Matthew, when all actuality, I wasn't. I was still in love with Raymond, however, being with Matthew filled the void.

One of the things that Matthew did that disappointed me was smoke weed. He kept pressuring me to get high with him. I explained to him that I already had experience with trying to smoke weed, eventually it would lead me back to crack. He kept trying to convince me that it was a mind thing and that I could handle smoking it as long as I only smoked when he smoked. My son Derrick and his girlfriend Diamond also smoked weed. I gave them all permission to smoke weed as long as it wasn't in my apartment.

I continued to go to meetings. I would share about how stressful it was living in an apartment with seven other individuals. Diamond and Derrick were constantly arguing, Myra and Myla were uncomfortable and Myra began acting out in school. My younger sons, Darrius and Michael seemed to be the only one who wasn't affected.

Matthew started acting different. I don't know if he was starting to think he'd made a mistake by leaving his wife, but things were getting tense between us. I was frustrated because Diamond wouldn't clean up after herself and Derrick. Myra and Myla were fighting with their brothers. The school started calling daily. It seemed that everyone in the house was stressing me out. All of a sudden I became overwhelmed. I took Matthew up on his offer and started smoking weed. After all, everyone else was happy and high, why shouldn't I be?

That again was a terrible mistake. Things changed really quickly. Within a couple of weeks, I went off and scored some crack, determined to smoke only once. Of course I was only fooling myself. I couldn't do "just one" of anything when it came to drugs and alcohol.

I didn't want to keep it a secret, so I told Matthew that I'd smoked some crack. He was upset, but he didn't leave me. Part of me started thinking this was a set up. I told him that I couldn't smoke weed because it would lead to me smoking crack, yet he still pressured me to smoke with him. I started thinking that it was his plan to smoke crack with me all along. It wasn't long before I'd spent all my cash. I asked Matthew if he would give me some money. He told me that he wasn't going to give me any money to buy crack with. So, I went to the drug dealer I'd been spending with and asked him would he front me some dope until I got paid the following week. Surprisingly, he did.

I came home and went into my bedroom closet and began smoking. Matthew was asleep or so I thought. He arose and asked me to give him a hit. I told him no. He kept saying just give me a hit! So, I consented and let him smoke some of the crack. After his first hit, he was off to the races.

One of the things I prided myself on was how although I'd been smoking crack, I made sure the bills were paid first, that we had food in the house, and that everyone had their needs met. Once Matthew and I both started smoking, things became unmanageable really quickly.

One day, Matthew told me to take off work for the day, get five hundred dollars out of the bank and rent a room. We were going to buy a lot of crack, weed and alcohol, have one final good time and then quit smoking crack. We did rent a room and smoked but we exceeded the five hundred dollars, and that was definitely not the last time we got high.

I quit my job the next week, for no other reason than it interfered with my using. My younger kids were still too young to realize what crack was, but they knew what weed was, so they assumed Mommy was smoking weed. Matthew and I began to argue a lot. He often accused me of having more dope after all the dope was gone. Or, he would say that I was smoking different crack giving him the less potent dope. He started hallucinating that there were other men in our bedroom hiding under the bed and that every time he turned his head they would give me crack cocaine.

It got really crazy. I didn't know that my son Derrick had started selling crack out the window of my apartment. I knew he was starting to sell weed, but didn't know he had begun selling crack and pills. I finally told Derrick that I was smoking weed. I didn't admit to him that I was smoking crack at first. He said he knew because it smelled like marijuana in my bedroom.

One evening, Matthew and I were in our bedroom just laying around, not really doing anything. He excused himself to go to the bathroom. After he'd been gone for ten minutes, I got up to see what was keeping him. As I was walking towards the bathroom, he was coming out. What was odd was the fact that the shower was running. He explained that he accidentally walked in as Diamond was in the shower.

I was livid. What type of fool did he take me for? He'd been gone for more than ten minutes. I suspected that he and Diamond were fooling around. What I also figured out is that he was getting crack from Derrick and paying him for it. I started wondering was Derrick letting him buy sexual favors from Diamond as well, after all, Derrick and Diamond led a really fast lifestyle. He allowed her to be a stripper for a long time, so I knew that he was aware that most strippers prostituted.

Matthew and I got into a heated argument. He swore to me that it wasn't what I was thinking. He kept saying it was a simple mistake. I decided to let it rest for the moment. Derrick's injuries, from the car accident, were still quite serious and I didn't want him to get angry and leave until he was completely healed, so I just held my peace for the time being.

Pretty soon Matthew's performance at work suffered tremendously. He started missing days to stay home and get high with me. His paychecks weren't as fat as they used to be. Sometimes he'd stay up all night getting high with me, and then go to work with crack-speckled, wrinkled clothing. Pretty soon, he was borrowing money from his co-workers and spending every dime he could get on crack. This wasn't what I bargained for. I knew I was hell on drugs, but he was a beast!

His supervisor called him in to the office. His supervisor happened to be the brother of my oldest daughter's father who knew my history with substance abuse. He asked Matthew was everything ok. He told Mathew he knew he left his wife to be with me and ever since his production at work decreased.

Matthew admitted to him that he'd started smoking crack, but he lied and said he was asleep and I blew the crack smoke in his mouth, that was how he ended up relapsing.

James' brother, Matthew's supervisor, called me the next day and asked me about it. I was pissed. I couldn't believe Matthew told that lie on me. Word got around the job quickly, and everyone had heard that I made Matthew relapse by blowing smoke in his mouth while he was asleep.

I was humiliated. Now everyone looked at me like I was the villain. My ex coworkers felt it was bad enough I'd ruined his marriage, now I had him strung out on drugs. Matthew also lied and told his sister in New York the same thing. She started asking him questions because she started wiring him money, and didn't know why all of a sudden he began needing money so often.

She called me and cursed me out, but later called to apologize when Matthew finally told everyone the truth. I was still upset, because I knew that deep down everyone would still believe I made him relapse and that he was just trying to cover for me.

After this things went completely down-hill. I'd finally admitted to Derrick that I was smoking crack. At that time he admitted to me that he was selling crack. As sick as it was, I started buying and getting crack from my son.

He would often give me more than what I paid for. I started losing weight at an alarming rate. I smoked all day and night. Matthew began asking Derrick to front him crack. We would often argue because when it came time to pay him, Matthew would try and put him off until the next pay day and go spend with another drug dealer. I wasn't having that. I told him that this wasn't any ordinary dope dealer he was trying to run game on. This was my son and we were going to do right by him. Once again, we would argue and fight over drugs and money. Our fights escalated from verbal to physical. My kids became frightened.

I started worrying that I would lose my kids again. I called my cousin Paulette and told her that I had relapsed and I needed to get some help, because I didn't want to lose my kids. She was disappointed but she asked me what she could do to help. I told her I wanted her to keep my kids for a week while I detoxed and I would start going back to my meetings. I begged her not to tell anyone. I was afraid that one of my family members would call CPS before I could get my plan in action. She agreed. We scheduled this to take place two weeks later.

Before any of this could take place, once again, I caught Matthew coming out of the bathroom while Diamond was in there. This time I snapped. I cursed them both out. Diamond was just looking at me not saying anything and Matthew was steadily trying to explain that he "accidentally" walked in on her again.

I went in the living room and told Derrick that those two kept ending up in the bathroom at the same time. Derrick wasn't fazed by this. I found it hard to believe he could be so calm about the situation. All he said is that he would talk to Diamond about it. That caused me to curse and scream even louder. I knew then that they were all playing me.

Matthew and I ended up getting into a serious fight. I told him he had to leave. He was begging me to understand that it was just an accident. Matthew's wife had moved out of their old apartment, but he still had keys to the place. I figured that was where he went. He stayed gone a couple of days. I can't really remember what I did during this time, but I noticed that Diamond wasn't happy at all. I was thinking it was because her little trick had to leave.

A couple of nights before I was scheduled to go to detox, Matthew called me and asked me if he could come and get me high. He said that he had a lot of money and he missed me. Of course, I wanted to get high, but I also missed him, so I met him at a convenience store and we went and scored. We spent the entire day getting high and having sex. As the day went on, my schizophrenia started flaring up. I started hearing voices. Once again, God and the devil were battling for my soul. I told Matthew that I couldn't do this anymore. He told me that I just needed to get some food in my stomach. After all, I hadn't eaten in two days. And, he thought eating something would bring me down.

On the way to Jack in the Box, Matthew started saying weird things. I knew that he was trying to spook me. I told him that he needed to stop, that I was already tripping. He thought it was funny and started laughing. By this time, we had our food. As he began to eat his burger, he looked over at me and said, "Boo!" I was so pissed that I told him to get out of my car. He started laughing hysterically. Finally, he saw that I was serious. He kept saying that he wasn't getting out and that I'd already put him out the house, there was no way he was getting out the car.

Rage boiled in my veins. I put my foot on the gas until it touched the floor. I rammed my car into a steel gate that surrounded a creek near my apartment. I hit it so hard that two windows shattered and the air bags deployed. I actually totaled my car. He was in utter disbelief. He told me later that I calmly walked away from the car eating my burger like "Carrie from the prom."

I made a phone call to the police and told them that I lost control of the wheel and to please send a tow truck for my vehicle. Things like totaling my own car and hurting myself thinking I'm hurting the other person has been a pattern for most of my life at this point. I'd heard it said that it's like cutting my own self and hoping YOU bleed.

After this, Matthew and I stayed away from each other for a couple of days. He was still working and therefore still had money, so he used his money as a bargaining chip to get back in the home. When he came back, I told him that we'd have to do better; otherwise I'd lose my kids again. I told him that I didn't need any help to lose them.

Things went okay for a while. Pretty soon, our crack habit spiraled out of control again. One particular night, we'd spent around four hundred dollars on crack. All we had left were ten measly dollars. Of course he wanted to spend our last ten dollars on getting one more, but I reasoned that we needed the money to wash clothes. I explained that the kids needed clean clothes to go to school and that he also needed clean shirts for work. He told me to wash the clothes by hand, because he was going to get some crack with the last ten dollars.

We argued about this for a while, finally I told him to keep his money. I started getting dressed in a mini skirt and low cut blouse, putting on makeup. He asked me where I thought I was going. I told him that I was going to make some money so that I could wash my kids' clothes. Matthew had been up without sleep for three or more days and I knew his thinking was screwed up.

We'd argued many times and have had some physical altercations, but never on the level of this night. He picked me up and threw me down on the ground and began hitting me in my face with his fist. I was trying to fight him back, but his blows were coming faster and harder. Finally, I ran to the payphone in the laundry room of the apartments I lived in. He chased me. As I'm on the phone with the police, he snatches it and attempts to choke me with the phone cord.

By the time the police make it to us, I am crying hysterically and he's holding me asking for forgiveness. The police saw my face and immediately put him in handcuffs. He went to jail for assault. He called everyday asking me to take a domestic violence class so that I could drop the charges on him. I talked to him by phone daily, but was already planning on how I was going to get out of this relationship.

I was depressed. Christmas was right around the corner. I had no money for gifts or even a tree. I made sure there was always food in the house and that the kids had clean clothes, but there was no extra money, and if there was, it was going on my crack.

A few days before Christmas, I was going through some old papers and I found a check from an insurance company that I didn't know was there. I sat it to the side months earlier thinking it was junk mail. I vowed to get gifts and a tree before smoking any crack or using alcohol.

Off to the shopping center I went. I bought a small tree and some decorations, each of the kids (including Diamond and Derrick) gifts, and a small turkey to cook on Christmas. As I unloaded everything, I made the kids leave out the room so they couldn't see their gifts. They were very excited. Pretty soon, the gifts were wrapped and the tree was decorated. They were happy that night. The next day, CPS knocked on the door.

I can't say that I was surprised, but I was hoping they wouldn't take my children. I talked with the investigator and told her the truth; I'd relapsed after having a tumultuous relationship. She seemed to be understanding and told me she wanted to get me some help, but that I needed to stay clean over the weekend.

I tried to stay clean, but the addiction was too powerful. I had a little money left over from shopping and I couldn't resist.

True to her word, the CPS investigator came back on Monday and drug tested me. I came up positive for cocaine. She had a form in her hand and gave it to me. It was an order to remove the kids from my custody. I went left. I told her there was no way she was going to take my kids with a simple sheet of paper, and that she better go and talk to a judge.

Because it was the holidays, I didn't think a judge would be available and that I could at least spend Christmas with my children. But, thirty minutes later she knocked at the door again with a court order and 3 policemen. I was about to lunge at her when Myla said "Mom no, we'll just go with her."

It truly broke my heart to see my kids leave once again. The saddest part was they didn't even cry. They just left like it was a matter of routine.

I sat alone in the apartment and for the first time in my life, I felt the self-hatred come with a vengeance. I hated myself. I hated my thought pattern, and the way I couldn't stop getting high. But, I hated Raymond as well. I hated him for making me love him with my whole heart, then destroying it. My self-esteem was so low, that I didn't think I was anything without him.

I was angry. Two days later, I woke up to cursing and objects being broken. Derrick and Diamond were in the living room fighting. I told them that they couldn't live in my house and fight. Diamond and I got into a huge argument and she called me a bitch. I called her mom and told her that Diamond could no longer live in my home and that she needed to come and get her or else she would be put out on the street.

Diamond's mother came to get her and Derrick left with her. He looked at me and explained that Diamond was his girl and he didn't want to choose. I told him to go ahead and go with her. Although we had gotten close, I didn't want him to feel like he was betraying me.

However, a couple of weeks later when I went to court for CPS, Derrick and Diamond had written statements saying that I would get high on drugs and start hallucinating that Diamond was having an affair with Mathew. I couldn't believe it. Now, THAT was a betrayal. I became angry with Derrick and didn't speak to him for almost a year.

I couldn't stop using at first. I was prostituting and getting high like it was nobody's business. I got a call from Mathew. He wanted me to pick up his last check and put money on his books. I thought he really must believe in me if he's asking me to do this for him knowing I'm in my addiction. I called the job to see when I could pick up the check. The secretary called one of the managers. The manager got on the phone and was being really cold to me. Although we knew each other personally and professionally, he treated me like a gold digger. He had heard the story that I made Mathew relapse and although Mathew later told the truth, he was one of the one's who still felt like I probably did make him not only relapse, but leave his wife as well. The manager told me that Mathew's last paycheck was going to his wife. So, I had Mathew get some power of attorney papers notarized that gave me the right to handle his affairs, up to and including, picking up and cashing his paycheck.

Everyone at the job was livid. His wife was furious. I picked up the check and cashed it. Out of it, I got a two hundred dollar money order that I had every intention of sending to Mathew. I started smoking with the remainder of the money and by the end of the next day; I had spent nearly two thousand dollars. The two hundred dollars never made it to Mathew. I cashed the money order and had another one drafted for one hundred dollars with every intention of sending that one. Of course, that one never made it either.

Pretty soon, the lights in my apartment were cut off. I started living like an animal again. There was no hot water or any way to heat water, so I stopped taking baths, only partially washing my body in cold water. I couldn't believe how low I'd sunk in such a short period of time. I would go visit the kids, and I would fall apart the minute I left. Guilt and shame were constant companions, so I needed to get high more often in order not to feel the pain of living with the fact that I'd once again lost my children.

I met a lady on the street and we started talking. She told me that she liked to get high also but didn't have a place to stay. She had a lot of drugs on her, so I told her she could come and live with me, but I explained to her I had no electricity or hot water. She said that was fine. It was almost like she whistled, because as soon as we agreed on the arrangement, out of nowhere her brother and two cousins walk up. They were all homeless and needed a place to stay, so they all moved in.

I used drugs with these people for a few months. They were professional panhandlers. I was amazed at their skill. They would tell elaborate tales to people who would give them cash, buy them food, and do whatever they could to help them.

I was still doing my best to keep up the rent, however, the rent got in the way of my drug use. Eventually, I was evicted and for the first time in my life, I became totoally homeless. I didn't have anywhere to go or no one I could call to sleep on their couch. After all, none of my family or friends were drug users, and I couldn't be trusted in anyone's home. I ended up downtown with a lot of other transients and homeless people. Before arriving downtown, I had a huge garage sale to get rid of my furniture and my kids' old toys and clothes. I cried that day thinking of how I was losing the things that I had worked for, selling the furniture that I'd bought when I was married.

When I arrived downtown, I had the few belongings I'd kept and had separated them into bags. I had a bag for my lingerie, a bag for shoes and purses, a bag for my hair products and make up, and a bag for my clothing. The other homeless people were looking at me like I was crazy. They were telling me that I was homeless and I had way too much stuff. They told me that all I needed is what would fit in a back pack. I began giving my items away. I was crying again, seeing transients walk around with my Doonie and Bourke purses, my Burberry shoes, etc. When I asked where I could plug up my flat iron the transients started laughing. They explained that now that I was homeless, I didn't have those luxuries. So, I hesitantly asked where do I use the bathroom....they looked at the dumpster and said, "We usually go behind there." That's when it hit me that I was actually homeless.

Being homeless took some getting used to. To the other transient people, I was an outsider and I was different than everyone else. I still wanted to take baths and groom myself, they were past the point of caring. Making money was hard. The tricks didn't pay well and I wasn't about to trick for ten or twenty dollars, so as a result, I missed a lot of money. One day I was incredibly hungry. I had no money, no dope, and no way to get either. I walked by a trash can and saw a food wrapper and wondered if there was food in it. I began rummaging through the trash looking for anything edible. Again, I began to cry, wondering how I had sunk so low. A few days later, I was arrested for drugs.

I was in jail, and I was happy. I had somewhere to lay my head, food in my stomach, and I was warm. I was almost disappointed when I went to court and received a 1244A which is a felony charge with misdemeanor punishment. I was released 2 weeks later. The moment I got out, I started hitchhiking. I wanted to get to my NA group by any means necessary. I wanted to try to live the NA way, I wanted to do anything but remain homeless. Although everyone was happy to see me, they were shocked to see the state that I was in. No one at my group had ever seen me that small. And although they were willing to help and buy me food and cigarettes, no one was willing to give me a place to stay. I ended up at an AA meeting and was riding with a guy who was also in recovery but didn't have very much time clean. Before arriving at the AA meeting, he rode through all the drug spots and I was scared he was trying to tempt me into using, so when we got to the meeting, I shared with one of the women that I had two weeks of sobriety and I was scared to continue riding with this guy. This woman, who was white not only took me in, but fed me and helped me out with clothing and toiletries. She also helped me get into treatment. While in treatment, I found out that a dear friend of mine I had met in recovery had been shot and killed while selling drugs. That also fueled me into the action of wanting to get better and stay clean.

Once again, I'd gotten out. I was still technically married on paper, but was estranged from Raymond. I found a small duplex with affordable rent and began the process of getting my children back again. I still didn't realize the affect that being uprooted from their house on several occasions had on my kids. I felt like when they were taken they were being taken care of and that was all that mattered.

Of course, I immediately found employment. For some reason, I was always able to get a good job. I was working, attending meetings, and was in the process of getting my children back for the third time. I bought a car and it seemed that I was well on my way. However, Raymond, seeing that I was once again doing well, came back into my life. This time, I was trying to stand for something. I told him that we would not be having sex unless we were working on getting back together. He told me that he loved me and that he did want us to get back together eventually, but that he was afraid I was going to relapse again, and that it took him a long time to get him and his daughter in their own place and back on their feet. So, of course we began sleeping together again.

Eventually the kids came home. By now they were getting older, and they weren't as joyous as I thought they'd be. They also weren't happy to see that I had taken back up with Raymond. They later explained to me that they felt abandoned by him as well as me. One day I received a call from a lady who told me that she and Raymond had a 3 year relationship, that her kids called him Daddy, and that they were planning on getting married. When I confronted Raymond, he confirmed that it was true, but that he told her he didn't want to divorce me; that he wanted to see if he and I could work things out. I gave him an ultimatum that night. I told him that he could either move me and my kids out of our little dank duplex or get us into a house where we lived as husband and wife or that I was going to file for divorce and move on with my life. A month later I filed for a divorce.

I attempted to move on with on with my life. I was rewarded custody of my children again, and I made a vow that I would find us a house and get us out of the little duplex we lived in. True to my word, I found a house which was privately owned by a white guy. I explained my situation and told him that I was in recovery, working, in college, and that I was a single parent with my kids. He felt for my plight and said he would help me. The first time I saw the house I knew I was home. It was absolutely beautiful. Although it was an older house, it had been completely remodeled. The bedrooms and closets were spacious and the hardwood flooring was bamboo. I couldn't wait for my kids to see the house. I had a feeling they would love it just as much as I did.

My feelings proved to be true. When my children saw the house they ran from room to room squealing and screaming. They were excited that we would have a nice big home to live in. I spent quite a bit of money decorating our home. I wanted to make sure their room was nice and that everything matched. We were happy for a long while. Everything was going great.

Eventually Raymond started stopping by. He said he wanted to make sure we were doing alright. Of course before long, we ended up sleeping together again. I couldn't find the strength to leave him alone. I even went to therapy. The therapist asked me what I wanted to gain out of therapy. I told him I wanted to gain enough strength to leave my ex-husband alone for good. The therapy was ineffective. I kept sleeping with Raymond, but it became so painful. He would have sex with me and then get up and wipe off and leave. He didn't stay to hold me or cuddle. He didn't stay to talk or communicate. It was almost like I was turning a trick.

I couldn't live like this anymore. I tried dating other guys. I even met a guy online named R.J., and at first he was cool. I thought I would be moving in a different direction. He told me that he smoked marijuana. Already having experienced being in a relationship where my partner smoked weed, I immediately told him that I was in recovery and that I couldn't be around it.

At first everything was cool. R.J. and I hung out a lot, but he never wanted to leave his apartment. He didn't smoke in front of me, but I always knew when he was high. One day we were sitting in his apartment playing dominoes when a guy came over. R.J. went into his bedroom and came back with a zip lock freezer bag full of weed. I knew then that I was in trouble. He was selling weed. I tried to ignore this fact, but it was awfully hard. I was hoping we would move in together, but I knew I couldn't have my children living in a home where drugs were being sold.

I began trying to get help. I didn't know what to do. I started sharing in meetings that the guy I was seeing sold weed. Not one person in my group came up to offer me advice or any suggestions. Instead they judged me and shook their head when I shared. By this time, I had fallen out with my sponsor, so I felt backed into a corner.

I knew that R.J. was no good for me, but I just couldn't stand the feeling of being alone. My kids were getting older and started acting up in school. They would act out when I left them at home so that I could work, and I started getting really stressed out.

The school started calling daily. I went to lots of parent/teacher meetings trying to discuss how we could work together to get the kids under control. Myra was especially acting up. I'd known that she'd always had issues, but I didn't realize they were more psychological than behavioral. I started whooping her every day the school would call. The whoopings got worse as she would continue to act out. At this time, I still didn't consider disciplining my kids as abuse. Besides, I grew up getting whoopings and after so many I would change my behavior, so I thought the same thing would work with my kids.

My resolve to stay clean started to weaken. I was overwhelmed with the kids behavior, and the fact that I was still hurting over Raymond. And, even though I was trying to move on, the new guy sold weed and our lifestyles didn't coincide.

Later that week, my brother and sister had a birthday party at a sports bar, so I went to hang out with them and wish them a happy birthday. While we were all hanging out, I told them that I was used to attending their parties and mentioned to them that I had never had a birthday party. They were the twins and their birthday was in the summer so growing up, they always had a party. They thought about this and were mortified. All these years of celebrating their birthday, they never gave any thought to the fact no one ever celebrated mine.

A few months later, my family threw me a birthday party. I had invited a few of my closest friends and I also invited Raymond. It was a nice party. Everybody I loved was there with the exception of Raymond. After the dinner, we went to a night club. Because of my issues with drugs and alcohol, I really didn't want to stay that long. I left the club early and went by Raymond's house. He pulled me in his arms and we had sex. After we'd finished, he looked at me and asked me what I was about to do. This was a hint that I was supposed to make my exit. I was heartbroken. I couldn't believe he wasn't going to at least spend the night with me on my birthday night.

I left his house that night with tears in my eyes. I went directly over to R.J's and asked him to roll me a blunt and make me a drink. He was concerned, but only briefly. He was already lit up. So, he said if that's what I wanted for my birthday, he would do it. He also told me that I never had to worry about weed. If I ever wanted to get high, just call or come by. I got high off weed and drank that night. I had two and a half years of sobriety at this time, and I smoked it up in a matter of minutes.

When I woke up the next morning I felt like a mack truck had run over me. My head was hurting and so was my stomach. I stayed in bed the next day. I took a few calls. I was almost sure my recovery friends could tell that I had relapsed, but no one noticed a thing. They talked to me like always. I began to secretly smoke weed and drink for the next five or six months.

During this time, I met another man at my group named Daniel. I was determined to leave Raymond alone and move on with my life; however, dating Daniel was a huge mistake. He was a maniac. He was verbally abusive and was always threatening me. I became scared of him. He tortured me and my children for months. He never hit us but he was always threatening to. I was still secretly using. I was so miserable. All I wanted was the safety of Raymond's arms. I missed him. I was sick without him. I wanted to date other guys to try and get over him, but it wasn't working.

Pretty soon, I started smoking crack again. This time, the drugs had me fooled. I was paying all my bills first, then using with what was left. I made sure my kids had food and clean clothing. The rent was paid, and my car note and insurance paid. The lights, gas, cable, and internet was paid. I thought I had found a way to successfully smoke crack.

My kids found out I was using because there was alcohol in my refrigerator. I sat them down and explained to them that

I had relapsed but that I wasn't going to lose them again. Their behavior escalated. The school kept calling every day about one or the other. At this time I was also in community college trying to get my degree. It was all too much. I started realizing that I couldn't get high and take my tests for school, so I started missing my test times. Pretty soon, I started falling behind in my school work. I was also working overnight in a call center, but eventually had to let it go as well. I couldn't work while I was high. My life once again seemed to be spiraling out of control.

I became angry. I was so angry that I no longer cared about anyone finding out that I was using. People at my group had already started suspecting anyway. My weight was dropping at an alarming rate, and my attitude had completely changed. It got to the point where I could no longer deny my drug use. I called the people closest to me in recovery, including my sponsor and told them that I was through with recovery. I told them that I was using and I was going to try and make it on my own, without the program. One of my friends told me that I was selfish and we got into a heated argument. I ended up hanging up the phone in her face, and began the process of slowly killing myself.

I started using more drugs more often. And, although the bills were getting paid, I found myself juggling them around, paying a little on this or that; just enough to keep the utilities on and food in the house. I ran into Raymond at our group. I really hadn't seen him or talked to him for a while and I was cool with that. I would do fine as long as he didn't call or try and talk to me. He came up to me and asked me if I wanted to gamble on his football board for the upcoming super bowl game by purchasing a square. The squares were twenty dollars apiece. Hoping my luck would change, I bought three. After handing him the money and choosing my squares, I hurried and walked away so he couldn't ask me about my relapse. Word had gotten around that I was using again.

Two days before the super bowl, I looked for my copy of the numbers and couldn't find it anywhere. I called Raymond and explained to him that I'd lost my paper. He told me I could stop by the next evening and pick up another.

The next evening I was riding around smoking weed when I remembered the football board. I called Raymond, told him I was on my way, and asked him to bring it outside. He told me that he'd hurt his back and was bed ridden and that I should just come in the house and get it. I was hesitant because I knew I smelled like marijuana.

When I walked in, his roommate was in the living room along with a few of his friends. I asked for Raymond and his roommate pointed to Raymond's bedroom and told me he was in the bed. I knocked on the door and went in. When I walked in, Raymond had the football board paper wrapped around his penis and told me to come and get it. I started getting angry. I couldn't believe his audacity. All I could think was that here I am still using and hurting behind our broken marriage, and the best he could offer was some more sex.

I told him that I didn't come for sex. I asked him for the paper. When he saw I wasn't going to play his game, he got up out of the bed and came behind me. He started grinding on me and asking me to "give him some." I said no repeatedly, but the more I said no, the more he rubbed and touched and groped on me. I had on a short skirt with a thong. He bent me over his bed quickly, pulled my panties to the side and rammed his penis inside me. I kept trying to get up, but he repeatedly pushed me down. I kept saying "Stop Raymond. I mean it, NO!" But, he wouldn't stop. I considered screaming, but I knew that if I did, he would never allow me at his house again. Ever mindful of this reservation, I didn't scream, but I was crying. I couldn't believe he was raping me like this. The fact that I had an orgasm fueled my anger even more. I felt that my body had betrayed me. I didn't want to have sex with Raymond. All I wanted was my paper and for him to leave me alone for good. Like always, he finished, wiped off, then asked me what was I going to do. I told him that it was fucked up what he did and that I didn't want him to speak to me ever again.

I cried all the way home. I wanted to call the police but instead I called his best friend who lived in Houston, Texas, and told him what happened and that I was about to call the police. His friend begged me not to. He asked me to give him a few minutes while he called Raymond and that he would call me back. He made me promise not to call the police yet. I promised I wouldn't. I sat there crying while he called Raymond. When he called me back, he reasoned with me to think about Raymond's daughter and how it would affect her if I put her father in jail. I asked him why I should think about his daughter. I told him that Raymond never thought about my children, he let them go to a shelter. His best friend told me that Raymond said if I didn't call the police, he would never bother me again.

Once again, my love for Raymond stopped me from making a police report. I wasn't alright. In fact, I was emotionally distraught.

The next week, the kids told me that there was water flooding in our laundry room. I went to check out the damage, and true enough, the pipe to my laundry room had burst and there was water everywhere. All the clothes we had strewn all over the laundry room floor were wet. Not to mention we had a pile of our dirty clothes still needing to be washed.

My landlord lived out of town. He told me it would take a couple of days before he could make contact with a plumbing company to make the repair. Not wanting the clothes to mildew, I piled up the kids and all the wet clothes in trash bags in my SUV, and set off for the laundry mat.

I stopped on the way and bought my kids McDonald's. I also got about sixty dollars in quarters to prepare to wash the clothes. As we loaded all the washers, my kids sat down to play their hand held video games and eat their food. I was angry. I had thirty four dollars to my name and I wanted to get high.

I told the kids I was going to run to the store to get fabric softener and to load the clothes in the dryer when they finished washing. Before leaving, I noticed a dopefiend I knew from the streets named Sherry. She had just gotten her clothes out of the dryer and was loading them into a trash bag. Not wanting to leave her there with my children (thinking she would jack them for their games or the money I'd left with them) I asked her if she needed a ride somewhere.

She told me she did and asked me to drop her off on Twelfth and Chicon, a street in a well-known drug area. I told her I was heading there anyway and wouldn't mind giving her a ride. She hopped in my vehicle and we drove to the streets. She and I were both searching for drugs. I took my twenty dollar bill and put it in my bra, and left the other fourteen dollars in my cigarette pack. By this time, I was seeing double. I had been up for ten days getting high and I was starting to feel it. I needed to get high in order to stay up to finish washing all those clothes.

I dropped Sherry off on the street and went home to get some fabric softener so that my kids wouldn't question why I didn't have it since that's what I left for. After leaving my house, I went back on Twelfth Street near the spot I'd dropped Sherry off moments earlier. I found a dope dealer who I usually tricked with and asked him to give me two for twenty. I promised him that I would come back and tighten him up if he did.

After scoring, I unlocked my vehicle and got in. I reached for my cigarette pack. Not only did it have my last fourteen dollars, it also had my brand new crack pipe. It wasn't there. I pulled my vehicle over and looked everywhere in the SUV, to no avail. I couldn't find it. I rushed back to the laundry mat where my children were. I told them I needed them to help me look for my cigarettes. By now, the clothes are finished drying and they are ready to head home.

I wouldn't let them get the clothes out of the dryer until we conducted a thorough search of my vehicle. The cigarette pack unfound, I was boiling over with rage. I told my kids to never mind the baskets and grabbed a box of trash bags and told them to hurry and fill them up with all the clothes. They kept asking what was wrong. I was crying and cursing and talking to myself. We finally got all the clothes bagged and loaded into my vehicle and made the drive home. On the way home, Myla, who was sitting in the front passenger seat, asked if I would please tell her what was wrong. I told her that the lady who I gave a ride to stole my money and that I was going to find her and stab her. I had no idea how insane it was to tell my daughter what I was about to do, but again, I had been up for ten days and I was furious. I wasn't thinking rationally.

When we made it to the house, I instructed the kids who were thirteen and nine that if I didn't make it home, they should get up and get dressed for school and someone would take them, more than likely Raymond. I went to my bedroom and grabbed a spare crack pipe, went to the kitchen and grabbed a knife, and wrapped it in towel.

On my way back to the block where I dropped Sherry off, I stopped at the store and filled up my gas can with gasoline. As I was moving doing all this, it started feeling like I was having an out of body experience. It was almost as if I was watching myself do all this.

When I made it to the street, I took an entire twenty dollar rock and put in on my pipe and hit it. While I was blowing out the smoke, I put the other twenty dollar rock on the pipe and hit it. I chunked the crack pipe out the window and jumped out the SUV with the gas can in one hand, and the knife wrapped in a towel in the other. I went to where Sherry was sitting and asked her where my cigarette pack was. She started talking noise and cursing at me saying she didn't take my damned cigarette pack. Her boyfriend was sitting there smoking a Newport cigarette and that solidified in my mind that they had my cigarettes.

I dashed him with the gas and struck my lighter attempting to set him on fire. He took off running and I even chased him for a spell, but it was obvious I wasn't going to catch up with him. Although he didn't catch on fire, the fumes did. It was enough to scare the hell out of him. I went back to Sherry. She was still sitting on the wall talking shit. I just attacked her. The first place I stabbed her was in the top of her head. I also stabbed her underneath her arm and on her arm. I went crazy. I was fighting her as well as stabbing her. A few of the drug dealers pulled me off of her. They couldn't believe I was going off like that. They always thought I was a perfect lady, never really bothering anyone. They began to plead with me to give them the knife. All I remember is that I was crying and kept saying over and over "Ain't nobody else gonna take nothing from me...." Finally, they got the knife out of my hand. One of the drug dealers went to get rid of it. There was a lot of blood when they pulled Sherry up from the ground. They didn't wait for an ambulance although someone shouted there was one on the way. Someone drove her to the hospital.

One guy told me to get in his van so that he could get me away from the scene of the crime. I was still having this out of body experience. I watched me get into the van and drive off with the guy. Later, I called R.J. to pick me up and take me to go get my vehicle. I told him what happened and he couldn't believe it. He kept saying someone had to have done something really bad to me for me to do that, because he just didn't see me going off like that for nothing.

I came home and checked on my kids who were asleep. I sat down for a minute trying to process what had happened. I still wasn't thinking rationally, but I also still wanted to get high. I decided to take a chance and go back to the streets to try and score some dope. I had a bag of marijuana R.J. had given me so I was going to trade it for crack. When I arrived at the scene before I could even get out my vehicle, it was surrounded by police.

They told me to step out of the SUV, so they could search both me and my vehicle. They found the weed and a crack pipe and told me that they were going to take me to jail as opposed to writing me a ticket, because some detectives wanted to talk to me about a stabbing that took place earlier that night. When I got to jail, I called Raymond and told him a little bit of what happened. I asked him if he would go by the next morning and take my kids to school. And, if I didn't get out for him to call my family and have them pick them up and keep them until I got out. On a whim, I decided to apply for a PR bond which is where they let you out on your word that you will come back to court.

I stayed overnight in jail and waited for the detectives to call me out. I was trying to think of a story I could tell, but

I was so hulled out and tired, my brain couldn't formulate a plan. I finally fell into a deep sleep. I was awakened two days later and was told that I had made bond. I kept asking where the detectives were that were supposed to be questioning me. No one seemed to have any answers, so I just went ahead and accepted the bond and got out of jail.

When I got out, I had several missed calls on my cell phone, so I started making phone calls. Everyone wanted to know what happened. Although I had slept for two days, I was still somewhat discombobulated. I was bragging about how I went on the streets and took care of my business. Most of my friends were in recovery and they were just dumbfounded as I explained to them how I stabbed Sherry.

I got out of jail on a Friday. My cousin had my children and refused to give them back. She said she had strict orders from CPS not to return the kids. Apparently, the kids went to school and told the front office they were scared because I went out to stab someone and didn't come home that night. The school, of course, called CPS and there was an investigation immediately.

I called my cousin and told her that I didn't care what CPS said, they didn't have custody of my kids; so by that Monday, have all their belongings with them at the school and I was picking them up.

I stayed at home by myself the entire weekend. I was still sneaking on the streets getting high, but the gravity of what I'd done started to hit me. I actually stabbed and hurt someone. By Sunday morning, I couldn't get out of bed. I woke up in the fetal position crying. The full measure of what I'd done had finally sunk in. I knew that I would probably be getting some prison time behind all this.

A CPS investigator knocked on my door that weekend. She wanted to talk about placing my kids somewhere until my legal problems were cleared up. I don't know if it was the drug induced state I was in or whether it was wishful thinking, but I somehow thought I could straighten the entire ordeal out without having to go to prison.

I resisted and rebelled against any suggestions the investigator came up with. For whatever reason, she didn't ask me to submit to a drug test. From the outside appearance of my house; big screen TV's, nice furniture, food in the refrigerator, I didn't seem to be using, but with the report given to them by the school, I'm sure drug use was suspected.

My kids were returned to me on the following Monday, and for two weeks we lived as if nothing was happening. I, however, walked on eggshells, thinking that any moment a knock on the door would come and the police would arrest me. I was still an emotional wreck as a result of the stabbing. One morning after getting the kids off to school, I began crying and worrying about going to jail. I decided to get up and clean my house to take my mind off the situation.

As I was cleaning my living room, I turned over the pillows in my couch to clean underneath them. I noticed a cigarette pack and picked it up. Lo and behold, there was the cigarette pack with the fourteen dollars and the crack pipe that I thought Sherry had stolen. Nothing I'd ever experienced in life had prepared me for the feelings I'd felt in that moment. Guilt and shame rose up in my throat like bile and flashbacks of blood and screams penetrated my brain.

I couldn't believe it. I had stabbed someone over taking something that wasn't missing. In my drug induced fog, I must've left the cigarette pack home when I made one of several trips to and from the Laundromat. I was devastated at this point. I didn't know how to fix this situation. I didn't know who to call or what to do.

I wanted to see if anything was reported on the police department's website, so I searched for my name. Upon conducting a search, I found out that I had a fifty two thousand dollar bond for a warrant for my arrest. I was sick. I contacted a lawyer who I heard would do favors for street girls who did sexual favors for him. I was willing to do whatever I had to do to avoid going to jail or prison.

The lawyer made an appointment with me for the following day. That night after the kids were asleep, I decided to spend my last twenty dollars on crack. I went back down to the same part of town where I'd stabbed Sherry and attempted to score. I'd left my vehicle parked on a side street and walked into a nightclub to make my purchase.

I saw a police car parked not too far from my vehicle. I knew in my spirit that he'd run my license plate and would probably arrest me as soon as I got into my vehicle, but the drugs were calling me, telling me that I could make it home without being pulled over. True to my initial thought, as soon as I drove off the police car followed and pulled me over.

I was taken to jail and booked for aggravated assault with a deadly weapon.

I can't begin to describe the sinking feeling I had in the pit of my stomach as I walked into the city jail. I knew that the day of reckoning had come and it was time to pay for the crime I'd committed. I still hadn't put together any days without using drugs, so I was still in a drug induced fog.

I thought that I would get off with probation, or even have the charges dropped altogether. I figured that the judge would compare my life to Sherry's life and see that I was obviously the victim. After all, I was a full time college student; I had a job, a house, and a nice vehicle. Sherry on the other hand was a known dope fiend and felon.

After being in jail for a couple of weeks, it became apparent that this was far more serious than I originally thought. I began praying, asking, no, begging God for mercy. I didn't want to lose my children again. I started thinking how the drugs had fooled me again. I thought that I was successfully using this time. Although my bills were paid and the children were clothed nicely and fed, I still ended up in jail. A passage from the NA literature constantly resonated in my mind, "…whose ends are always the same…jails, institutions, and death."

As I prayed each night, I wanted to plea bargain with God. I would cry and pray and explain to God how I wasn't in my right mind at the time of the incident and tell him he knew it. Finally, I saw my court appointed attorney. Coincidentally, I was also seeing an attorney appointed to me by the family courts for the children. I felt like I was being hit with a double whammy. I was being tagged team by both systems, and I felt more powerless than I'd ever felt in my life.

Eventually, my criminal attorney told me that I was going to be doing some time. They were trying to give me a 15 aggravated year sentence. I couldn't believe it. That would mean that I would do the more than half the time. I couldn't see being away from my children for 8 years. I went to court several times over the course of 7 months. I kept refusing the time offers. I honestly didn't want any time. I wanted God to forgive me and let me out.

Every time I went to court, it was surreal. We submitted a "Motion to Discover" and found that in the original police report the initial stab wound was listed as a contusion. They went down from 15 aggravated to 2 years aggravated. The lawyer suggested that I take it. She assured me that they were not going to give me probation. I wanted to take it to trial. I knew the jury would want to see the weapon and they didn't have it.

The lawyer told me to think about it over the weekend and on Monday I needed to let her know what I was going to do. That night I prayed and asked God once again for mercy. I began to cry and ask God why I had to do time, why couldn't he just let me go home with lesson learned? God spoke to my heart that night. He said, "Because you did it." It was in that moment that I felt the presence of God. I knew that I could do the time. I didn't want to, but I had to accept the fact that even though I wasn't in my right mind, I still committed the crime. I put myself in the position for everything to happen.

By this time, CPS had taken me to court over the children. My aunt volunteered to take the children in while I went to do time, so they didn't take away my parental rights as they were originally trying to do. I was grateful. I didn't want to lose my parental rights to my children.

While I was in jail, Raymond was over my money. He would put money in my inmate trust fund and came to visit me. I was in love with him still, but I couldn't go back to the way things were before. I vowed I would make a change during my time of incarceration. By the time I "pulled chain" to prison, I heard from Raymond less and less. I cried for my kids every day. I thought about the birthdays and school years I would miss. I thought about how we had moved into a beautiful home and once again, I messed it all up. I read the bible and prayed daily for strength. Two things I knew for sure: I didn't want to put my hands on anyone anymore in violence, and I didn't want to use drugs. The spiritual price tag was much too high.

While in prison this time, I stayed to myself. I didn't watch TV or play dominoes. I read a lot of self-help books and my bible. I wrote poetry, wrote in my journal, and I prayed. I felt confident that I was getting my rage and other issues under control, however, during the holiday season, a few of the white girls were fooling around and smeared black paste made of coffee and water on their faces. They were pretending to be Black, saying that it was "Black Friday."

They did a skit that I found very offensive. I sent another inmate over to them to ask them to remove the coffee from their face and stop doing their skit. One of the ladies, a twenty one year old girl, made a sarcastic remark and once again the inherent rage that lives within me boiled over. I jumped off my bunk and ran up to her and just started beating her. I was beating her so badly the guards wouldn't even break us up. Later they told me that I was fighting so furiously they were afraid to get in it. I beat this little girl so badly; she had two black eyes for about three months.

I only stopped hitting her because I finally heard her begging me to stop. I immediately felt like a monster. I couldn't believe I'd beat this child up. I was appalled at my behavior. I thought after I'd stabbed Sherry I was finished with the violence. I wanted to change, but I didn't know how. I didn't know where the rage would come from. I didn't understand why I couldn't control my emotions and not resort to violence. I was sick of me.

Chapter 5

Healing

"You can fill your life with if only's or you can get on with it..... In my family, we get on with it."

-Judy Blume
"Summer Sisters"

I entitled this chapter "Healing." Not "The solution," "Cured," or anything that states finality. Healing implies a process over time. Merriam Webster defines healing *to cause an undesirable condition to be overcome.*

Although, I am still a work in progress, I think about my last act of violence in jail, and my emotional and spiritual state at that time. After beating the twenty one year old girl while in prison, I began praying earnestly, asking God to change me. Asking him to help me with whatever it was that caused me to go into such tumultuous fits.

In prison, psychiatry is sporadic and impersonal. You meet with the psychiatrist once a month, but only general questions are asked, and they only expect general answers. On one of my routine visits to the psychiatrist, I told him that I needed some intensive help. He broke protocol and asked what was going on. I had an opportunity to explain my condition and severe bouts of rage. He became concerned and asked me were my meds effective. Basically, mostly everyone in prison was on the same types of medication. They don't customize meds unless you are allergic to a particular kind of medication.

He took an interest and worked with me for the next couple of weeks, adjusting and readjusting my meds until I started feeling better. He began pulling me out weekly, talking with me and discussing my history and other extenuating circumstances in my life that led me to this point.

Pretty soon, I was getting excellent mental health care. I was able to do some work on anger management and coping skills. I learned that the issues I suffered from were so deeply rooted that the things in my present actually reminded me of things from my past because I had never dealt with those issues.

I started feeling better about my life. I continued to read my bible and pray, and started making a plan for my life. I knew that God had a greater purpose for me than what I'd been doing for the last thirty years.

Eventually, I started attending NA meetings in prison. When I walked into my first meeting, I knew that the NA program was my permanent solution. I started working the steps in prison and really taking a look at my life.

I knew that if I wanted to live.....truly live, I had to surrender my perception of the world and the people in it. But mostly, I had to stop using my past as an excuse to destroy my present and future.

I began ordering books on mental illness and its effects. I started understanding that I suffer from a dual diagnosis. Not only am I mentally imbalanced, I also suffer with the disease of addiction. The two are inherently intertwined. The **major** illness is, of course, the mental illness. Drugs were also a major problem, but mainly a way to self-medicate. However, it also caused a further chemical imbalance. I knew that I had to find out exactly what I suffer from or else I'd be doomed to repeat the same insanity.

The psychiatrist performed an extensive family history research and it dawned on me that mental illness was severe on both my paternal and maternal sides of the family. I learned that a lot of what I suffered from had a lot to do with genetics. I found relief in this revelation. I didn't want to be a bad mother or a bad person. I didn't want to make harmful decisions and hurt the people who love me most.

Another realization I had was the fact that one of the symptoms of bipolar disorder was that once I began taking medication and would start to feel better; I'd think I wouldn't need the meds anymore. For years, I had to tape a sign to my bathroom mirror that said, *"You feel better because you're taking your meds dummy!"*

I had to also find out the meaning of true surrender. I'd known for years that drugs were a major problem. And, once I found recovery, I knew I'd found a way to get clean. However, I couldn't stay sober for more than a few years.

A member of recovery broke down the way surrender works. When you surrender, you actually surrender *to* something. If you're not surrendering *to* something, then you're just *resigning*. It finally sunk in. All the times I would come back and try to stay clean, I had only *resigned* because every time I relapsed, I'd lost an exhausting battle with drugs.

I learned to surrender the belief that I could have *"just one"* or that I could ever use successfully. I began to love myself. When I'd learned to love myself, I knew that I was worthy of living drug-free.

I finally understood that most mothers who repeatedly fail at effective parenting usually suffer from issues that are greater than they are. What became most apparent is the fact that the disease of addiction was greater than the love I have for my children. I also realized that I had to take excellent care of my mental health, taking prescribed medication as directed by a mental health professional and participate and fully engage in intensive therapy. I knew my mental health had to be my number one priority along with staying drug-free since untreated mental illness is a major factor in substance abuse.

In order to combat the disease of addiction, I had to connect with a power that was greater than it. So I learned to trust and have faith in God. I didn't know how to a first. I felt angry at God for allowing all those bad things to happen to me. I was even angry because I felt God made me the way that I am.

On some days guilt and shame overwhelm me. For years I've been stuck in the cycle of "good intentions-messing it all up-regret". That cycle has repeatedly played over and over in my life. I've mostly felt disappointed that I haven't been the mother that I always wanted to have.

I started searching for something to help me combat those feelings of self-loathing and remorse.

For my mental health, I had to have a targeted prospectus in combating the issues I suffered. I want to share what works for me.

- Ongoing assessment for sexual abuse history.
- Treatment addressing trauma issues.

- Treatment for comorbid (more than one altogether) mental disorders.
- Treatment addressing family dynamics and support.

For me, mental health is only a part of what I needed help with. Spiritually, I was sick. Neither money nor material wealth can heal me. It took many years to realize that my spirit cannot be healed by such. The "right" man or the "right" set of social and economic circumstances couldn't heal me either. There is a hole in my spirit that only a loving God can fill.

I had to look back over my life and see it was God that kept me and protected me from death all those times I should have been dead. But mainly, God protected me from myself. When everything in me wanted to die, he persistently instilled in me the will to give it one more try.

Today, I truly believe that God has chosen me to break cycles of abuse in my family and in my community at large. I no longer feel the rage I once did. I continue to seek therapy for unresolved issues, stay in the 12-step process, and worship my Lord and Savior Jesus Christ.

Chapter 6

Exposing the Silent Epidemic

"Someone was hurt before you, wronged before you, hungry before you, frightened before you, beaten before you, humiliated before you, raped before you... yet, someone survived... You can do anything you choose to do."

-Maya Angelou

In order to fulfill my desire to publish this book, I knew my story alone was not enough to provoke the change I'd like to see take place in our communities. In truth, I feel that if I can help make a difference in the life of one person, my mission is complete.

I knew I had to research the subjects of molestation, addiction, and mental illness as it relates to African Americans. Not that African Americans are the only ones who suffer in these areas, just that I happen to be African American and born into a culture whose national anthem is, ***"What goes on in this house stays in this house."*** I feel, based on my own experience, this golden rule is sure to get someone killed or cause more of our children to be abused, molested, and become damaged adults who abuse and neglect their children as well and further perpetuate the cycle.

As it relates to Molestation:

[1]*Although children of every gender, age, race, ethnicity, background, socio economic status and family structure are at risk, race and ethnicity are an important factor in identified sexual abuse. African American children have almost twice the risk of sexual abuse than white children.*

According to studies, there are more African American related cases of sexual abuse than any other ethnic group. I found this to be paradoxical since those same studies show that those cases often go unreported. Although it baffles me as to how they came up with this estimation, many

---

[1] Sexual Abuse (Darkness to Light.org),

researchers believe that it is because African Americans are used to bearing pain in a predominantly discriminatory society. They believe African Americans often view acts of molestation and abuse as somewhat a general course of life.

Child molesters of any ethnic group mainly molest children close to them. 85-95% of reported cases of sexual abuse involve a perpetrator known to the child, 35% involve a family member, and 50% of all sexual assaults take place in the home of the child or offender. The average offender is involved with over 70 children in his or her offending career.

Although sexual offenders have various circumstances that cause them to perpetrate, research shows that sexual abuse is mainly a "learned behavior" meaning they themselves were at one time victims of sexual abuse.

As it relates to Physical Abuse:

Recent studies have shown that 89% of African Americans spank their children. Although people from other ethnic groups have been known to spank their children as well, most of those people have often spanked with an open hand, whereas African Americans often use an object, sometimes dangerous ones.

Some researchers believe that harsh whippings are a legacy "left by the brutality of slavery". Other researchers believe that African Americans have a more rigorous religious belief that reinforces the old saying "Spare the rod, spoil the child".

At any rate, a lot of times, spankings in our culture often border or cross the line to child abuse.

Statistics show that 95% of child abusers were abused themselves as children. The cycle seems to repeat itself when those victims of abuse have children as well.

Based on my personal experience, it is no longer acceptable for me to spank my children. Spankings and beatings were deeply entrenched in my psyche as the ultimate form of discipline that would bring about a desired result but because of my mental health issues, I couldn't differentiate the fine line of spankings and abuse.

I have also come to believe that it is impossible for me to teach my children that hitting someone or being hit by someone is unacceptable if I, myself, am hitting them.

As it relates to Addiction:

[2]*High risk factors for substance abuse disorders for African Americans, particularly the youth population include low self-esteem, low levels of family pride, and deviant peer associations. A family history of alcoholism has also been found to be a significant predictor of substance abuse for this population.*

Some minorities experience pervasive stress unique to their minority status that may contribute to their drug use, such as pressure to reconcile values of their culture of origin

---

[2] OSAS Retreatment of African Americans

with those of mainstream American culture. Racism, discrimination, language barriers, and dealing with social service agencies have been associated with substance abuse disorders within minority populations.

For African American adolescent males in particular, drug dealing appears to be a significant risk factor for developing a substance use disorder.

Research demonstrates strong evidence between drug use, drug dealing, and homicide for the African American population.

This summation mirrored my own opinions in this regard to substance abuse. During my time living the street life, I was surrounded by young drug dealers, who themselves were addicts unbeknownst to them. They would smoke weed (which is now a days chemically enhanced), pop pills, and smoke wet (embalming fluid). The money they make dealing crack cocaine mainly goes to supply their own drug of choice. Jails and institutions are flooded with such type of young, Black males. They are also often gang related and get into turf wars with other gangs, which add to the homicide rate. Nearly half of all prisoners in the United States are African Americans. This is a vicious cycle that I hope one day will end.

As it relates to Mental Illness

[3]*The most common mental disorders involve depression, with nearly 20 million Americans suffering some form of*

3

http://www.theroot.com/articles/culture/2013/05/mental_health_illn

major or mild depressive disorder. According to the **_National Institute of Mental Health,_** *"Most likely, depression is caused by a combination of genetic, biological, environmental, and psychological factors. "Additionally, "Some genetics research indicates that risk for depression results from several genes acting together with environmental or other factors. In addition, trauma, loss of a loved one, a difficult relationship, or any stressful situation may trigger a depressive episode."*

With Black Americans leading the country with troubling statistics in areas like **unemployment, child abuse and neglect,** *and* **domestic violence,** *all of which can exacerbate stress, it is perhaps not surprising that the community leads the country in mental health struggles. According to the Center or Disease Prevention's* **_Office of Minority Health and Health Disparities_**, *African Americans are "still more likely to experience a mental disorder than their white counterparts "but less likely to seek treatment" though* **_Psychology Today_** *recently noted that there has been an increase in the number of Black Americans seeking treatment for ailments such as depression over the last decade. Men are less likely to seek treatment than women, regardless of race, meaning Black men are the least likely to seek treatment over all.*

Upon researching mental illness as it relates to African Americans, I was amazed at some of the facts I learned. With all the advancement in mental health care, it still

---

ess_in_blacks_failure_to_seek_treatment_may_be_holding_us_back. html

plagues me why many more Black Americans do not seek out mental health care.

Another alarming mental health issue amongst Black Americans is bipolar disorder. Bipolar disorder, also known as Manic Depression, is an illness marked by severe mood swings-phases of euphoria and often depression. It is sometimes accompanied by schizoaffective disorder, a condition that includes chronic symptoms of schizophrenia and also episodes of affective disorder (either bipolar or depressive). This illness often goes undiagnosed and undetected in many Americans.

[4]While the rate of bipolar disorder is the same among African Americans as it is among other Americans, African Americans are less likely to receive a diagnosis and treatment for this illness because:

- A mistrust of health professionals.
- Cultural barriers between doctors and patients.
- Reliance on religious community during times of emotional distress.
- **<u>A tendency to mask symptoms with substance abuse.</u>**
- No health insurance. (25% of African Americans don't have health insurance).
- Continued misunderstanding and stigma about mental illness.

From my own experience, while I was academically gifted and creative in many ways, I have always struggled

---

[4] NMHA.org

socially and emotionally as a result of my diagnosis of bipolar with schizoaffective disorder. And true to the fact stated above, I often masked my symptoms with drug use. I feel that the substance abuse further accelerated my chemical imbalance.

Other facts I discovered:

- [5]African Americans are disproportionately more likely to experience social circumstances that increase their chances of developing a mental illness.
- Children in foster care and the child welfare system are more likely to develop mental illnesses. (African American children comprise 45% of the public foster care population.)
- Nearly half of all prisoners in the United States are African American. Prison inmates are at a higher risk of developing a mental illness.
- Exposure to violence increases the risk of developing a mental illness. (Over 25% of African American children exposed to violence meet criteria for posttraumatic stress disorder.)

These facts were eye-opening for me. I realized how important my mental health was in regards to making healthy decisions for me and my children. It is important for us as Black Americans to seek mental health care. I believe this would alleviate some of the disparity we have in association to our children in foster care, our children abusing substances, and also passing down our misguided

---

[5] National Alliance on Mental Illness (NAMI.org)

beliefs to our children, furthering the cycle of misinformation.

Many African American women who have suffered sexual abuse general have more suicidal thoughts and/or attempts, greater histories of inpatient mental health institutions, more years of cocaine use, and more problems due to substance abuse.

Many coping behaviors they use are: problem avoidance, wishful thinking, social withdrawal, and self-criticism. African American women with sexual abuse histories also have a more complex clinical picture. They have more severe psychiatric symptoms, more complex family histories, and more experience of a range of traumas.

We must begin the process of getting better by reevaluating our belief systems. Culturally, our belief systems have been passed down from generation to generation, and while we at some point upgrade these symptoms, our core beliefs traditionally center on those that were handed down.

Warning Signs of Sexual Abuse

- *Sudden change in mood or behavior.*
- *Trouble walking or sitting.*
- *Displays knowledge or interest in sexual acts inappropriate to his or her age, or even seductive behavior.*
- *Makes strong efforts to avoid a specific person without reason.*
- *An STD or pregnancy, especially under the age of fourteen.*

- *Runs away from home.*

Behavioral Signs of Sexual Abuse

- *Uncomfortable around or rejection of typical family affection.*
- *Problems in school.*
- *Reports of sexual assault.*

If you, or someone you know is the victim of child-hood sexual abuse you may contact:

National Child Sexual Abuse Hotline

Darkness to Light

1-866-FOR-LIGHT (866-367-5444)

Or

Stop It Now

1-888-PREVENT (888-773-2362)

Or

The Childhood National Child Abuse Hotline

1-800-4-A-CHILD (800-422-4453)

For help with alcohol or chemical dependency call:

Alcohol and Drug Helpline (800-821-4357)

Alcohol and Drug Abuse Hotline (800-729-6686)

National Council on Alcoholism & Drug Dependence Hopeline (800-622-2255)

For a Mental Health Crisis

National Mental Health Association 800-969-NHMA (800-969-6642)

EPILOGUE

I wrote this book while in prison doing a 2 year sentence for aggravated assault with a deadly weapon for stabbing Sherry. I vowed while in prison not to play dominoes all day or sit around and tell war stories. I made a plan for my life and swore that I would do whatever I had to do to address my mental issues, gain closure on my past issues, and avoid drugs and the "street" lifestyle altogether.

*At the time of the publishing of this book I have formed a non-profit organization **Remember To Think Pink** whose mission is to increase awareness of debilitating issues that hinder effective parenting through research, community service, parent/child programs, and advocacy. It also serves as a reminder to parents to remember my story in "The Pink Elephant in the Middle of the Getto" before making decisions that will alter the life of your child.*

I continue to progressively work a 12-step program, see mental health professionals, and express myself through spoken word poetry. I am seeking a degree to become a forensic social worker, and I am dedicated to stopping the progression of child neglect and abuse by working with parents. It is my belief that in working with parents, the children are automatically and consequentially helped as well.

I am currently in the process of being afforded the privilege to work CPS services and gain custody of two of my children for the fifth time. I am well aware that there is nothing "cute" about that and it is unfortunate that my children have suffered while I have struggled to find healthy mental and emotional balance. I am grateful that in spite of my own decisions my children have persevered and are becoming healthy young adults.

My message is NOT that you are able to continuously make bad decisions and be able to get your children back five times... My message is that you never have to lose your children, and if for some reason you have....you never have to lose them again.

Acknowledgements

As it pertains to this book and my life work, there are so many people to thank. I first of all thank the God of my understanding who enabled me to make it through this living hell and is allowing me the privilege to be a living testimony to others. A special thank you to my sponsor Kim W. and my therapist John W. who together keep me mentally and emotionally balanced.

I thank my brother D. R. Cleveland and my beautiful sister n' law Sheron who have stayed up many nights listening, supporting, encouraging, praying, and fussing and who opened their home and hearts and allowed me to pursue my dreams.

I want to especially thank the women at Dawson State Jail who read as I wrote and kept me motivated by telling me what my writing was doing for them emotionally; a special thank you for Unique M. and Chuncy Y. You two were my ultimate sounding boards.

I want to thank the members of my NA home group who over the years have helped me, supported me, and believed in me, especially Myron B., Kim W., and Douglas E.

I want to thank my church family, giving special recognition to my Pastor Rev. Edward M. Fleming Sr., the Olivet Baptist Church choir- who prayed for me and with me, and my spiritual mentors Sister Gloria Smith and Sister Grace Reeves. I also want to thank my editor and my literary mentor and sister in Christ, Rose Chase Smith who is truly an inspiration to me.

Thank you to my Greenstream International family and coworkers who supported events, gave me ideas, and listened to my endless chatter giving a special shout out to the ladies in HR who have "mothered" me. I thank this company who gave me a chance to become a productive member of society when all other doors were closed.

I want to thank my family who loves me and supports me in my efforts and who have continuously kept faith in God. To my aunts, sister, brothers, cousins, nieces and nephews, thanks for loving the real me. Since all of you have been there for me at different parts in my process, it's hard to single out any one of you, but I would be remiss not to thank my cousin Katonya who loves me like a sister and my niece Keyanna who loves me like a mother.

I'd like to give a special thank you to the love of my life and prayer partner Vincent; the man who stays up with me all night on the phone, listening and fine-tuning my ideas. The first man who recognized, appreciates, and reminds me daily of my gifts.

Lastly and MOST of all, I'd like to thank my children who have been patient, strong, trusting, forgiving and have never stopped loving and believing in me. You guys motivate me, inspire me, and are the very reason I have never, will never, give up.

For each book I sell, a portion of the proceeds will go towards launching #TeamTiTi. A financial resource that helps offset the cost of counseling for children who've been neglected or abused.

CPSIA information can be obtained at www.ICGtesting.com
Printed in the USA
LVOW10s1835190916

505261LV00019B/1364/P